Period & CONTEMPORARY

Patterns for Fashion Dolls

by Hazel McMahon

Published by Hobby House Press, Inc.
Grantsville, Maryland
www.hobbyhouse.com

Dedication

I'd like to dedicate this book to the memory of May Wells Agnew, my Gran, who patiently taught me to knit, crochet and sew. She would have just loved these fashion dolls, covering their clothes in jewels, just as she did my first *Barbie®* dolls. And for my dad Ian, who just understood everything—even my "doll thing"— without reservations.

Acknowledgements

First, a big thank you to my long suffering husband, Hugh, and my kids, Christopher, Kimberley and Nicole, for tolerating me and not having a cooked dinner for months. Thanks to my mum for helping me with the "boring bits" of sewing. Also, thanks to my dear friend and fellow Scot, Anne-Marie Burns, for just being there when I needed support and an ear as I croaked over the phone. Thanks to Mary Beth for her beautiful fabrics and ribbons, which are so hard to obtain here in the UK, and for being a friend. Finally, thank you to the doll designers and creators for providing such wonderful canvasses with which to work and stretch our imaginations.

Additional copies of this book may be purchased at $26.95 (plus postage and handling) from
Hobby House Press, Inc.
1 Corporate Drive, Grantsville, MD 21536
1-800-554-1447
www.hobbyhouse.com
or from your favorite bookstore or dealer.

©2001 by Hazel McMahon
1st Reprint—March 2002

Printed in the United States of America

ISBN: 0-87588-608-6

Table of Contents

Tips on Resources and Supplies

RESEARCHING COSTUMES:

I always find that this is the most exciting part of the whole process of creating an outfit for any particular doll. Since most of today's fashion dolls have a certain identity, it's easy to home in on a certain era or time period to research. Obviously we can buy or borrow books on costume and fashion, but there are other avenues that can prove to be most useful.

There's the Internet for one. One can use a search engine and spend a whole day perusing the sites, which offer pictures and information on yesterday's and contemporary fashions. Later I list a few that I find useful. Auction sites are also quite useful. There you can look at authentic vintage clothes, hats, purses and shoes, and save the pictures that interest you most building your own fashion library.

Magazines such as *Vogue*, *Harpers Bazaar*, *Glamour*, *Mademoiselle*, and *French L'Officiel*, dating from the early teens right through to modern day with their wealth of fashion spreads are a natural source of inspiration. For 20's and 30's clothing, look to fashion magazines such as *Weldon's* or *The Delineator*, which have wonderful hand-drawn illustrations, and can be picked up relatively cheaply. This is also true of pattern books such as *McCall's*, *Butterick* and *Vogue*. Advertisements in these publications are also helpful in that they show accessories and how women were "sold" on an image be it Clara Bow's hats in the twenties or Lana Turner's nylons in the forties.

Vintage sewing patterns also give up the secrets of just how to cut and drape some of those ingenious styles of the 30's and 40's and are relatively inexpensive at sales or from the numerous companies now dealing in vintage ephemera. Vintage paper dolls can also be an invaluable source of costuming, showing current fashion styles, and colours of the time. Many show complete wardrobes.

For earlier costumes, look to museums and art galleries for portraits of titled and society ladies. Most establishments now provide postcards and catalogues with such illustrations. Many great works of literature, such as *Pride and Prejudice*, have been serialized for television and film; these also provide a wealth of costume ideas that cover all areas of class and society, from lowly servant attire to costumes worn by a titled lady at court.

Then there are the movies—celluloid fashion according to Hollywood. One can see how women dressed throughout the decades, both day and evening wear, attired by Hollywood's best designers—Adrian, Travis Banton and Edith Head to name a few. However, as with all make-believe, when recreating those earlier costume dramas, especially those made in the forties and fifties, historical accuracy went out the window (a cringing Scot here thinking about *Brigadoon*!) But then the world at that time needed escapism of a colourful kind, and that's just what Hollywood supplied.

So you can decide whether you want to be historically accurate with your design or if you want to romanticize your ideas, just like a Hollywood designer. Pure escapism! No rules. . . just fun.

FABRICS:

Where possible, use natural fabrics for dolls clothes i.e. silk, cotton, lawn, silk satin, taffeta, fine woolen crepes and tweeds, and cotton laces. The end result will certainly reflect your choice.

One thing you must remember though is scale. In the end, you'll be glad you did. Scale is of the utmost importance when choosing patterns on fabric or laces. Craft cottons have wonderful tiny patterns, but they should be chosen with care, as they tend to always look like "craft" cottons! Remember, each period had it's own styles in fabrics and colours, so try to be sympathetic to your chosen design. Research your outfit through old magazines, costume books and period films.

When searching for fabrics remember the thrift stores for vintage fabrics, avoiding soiled or musty fabrics. If possible, launder your finds before cutting and sewing incase of shrinkage when steam pressing, or worse still, dye bleeding onto your vinyl doll. Also consider the weight (thickness/thinness) of your fabric. Don't ask it to do something it can't or won't lend itself to i.e. a woolen tweed would be like a carpet on a doll—too stiff and bulky! Choose the finest or lightest weights possible in all fabrics. Whether it be silk or a wool cloth, it will effect the hang and drape of your finished garment. So too with linings. These must be sympathetic to your main fabric and not add bulk or act like a cardboard stiffener unless you want that look say in a collar, hat, or corset. Instead of using heavy velvet, consider using knit back velvet or velour, which takes darts and tiny seams without adding bulk. Stores that supply miniature bear making supplies have a very fine upholstery velvet that has a fray free backing and comes in a wide variety of miniature prints and solid colours. These fabrics are invaluable for doll hats, bags, collars, cuffs, or contemporary faux fur skirts and pants. They also sell Ultrasuede, a fine pliable man-made mock suede, in a variety of colours. It's also wonderful for hats, purses, and tiny appliqué trims.

Don't overlook felt! Its firmness lends itself to hat or purse bases, or for non-fraying appliqué motifs, but it has a tendency to stretch.

You can create your own fabric. Piece together small pieces of fabric just like vintage quilts and embroider onto them. Then cut and sew. Sew coordinating bands of fabric together and you'll have an instant striped garment piece if cut and aligned correctly.

COLOUR, TEXTURE, WEIGHT:

The correct combination of all three can make or break your outfit. Before cutting and sewing anything, create little "themed" piles of fabrics. Gather a variety of coordinating colours in different types of fabrics. Then mix textures—a rough with a smooth, a thick with a thin. Bag all these piles for future use, popping in beads or trims, which fit the "theme". Don't be afraid to experiment with colour combinations. For instance, add a hint of orange to that turquoise pile even if the colour is only picked up in the accessories. Be daring, and if you don't feel you have the confidence to experiment, make a scrapbook of ideas on colour that excite you. Look at photos of nature, cut up magazines, and save fashion photos. You can borrow from these examples when you need inspiration. Textile and clothes designers get there inspiration in the same way, paying a kings ransom to forecasting companies who supply the annual season's themes, normally a few years in advance.

TRIMMINGS:

Look for small trims, buttons, laces, and beads that could be incorporated into your project. Men's silk or rayon ties are a gold mine of miniature prints and brocades that can be used as collars or for purses and other accessories. Vintage scarves and head-squares are also great.

Children's clothes and their trims lend themselves to dolls clothes as well. The coloured faux fur trim on that infants ski suit as a dolls wrap and party clothes can be recycled into classy evening dresses! Just keep an eye open for the unusual. Remember there are no rules. Use what you can to achieve the look. Local stores selling ribbons, beads, feathers etc. can be a glut of material right under your nose if you just look around.

Antique markets, shows and thrift shops are full of materials waiting to be reused i.e. laces, crocheted doilies, embroidered linens, discarded beaded oddments. Old earrings can be reborn as miniature purses, as doll brooches or pins, chains for purse straps—whatever your imagination can create. Break down unusual necklaces and reuse the beads. Old and unusual buttons, buckles, broken jewelry can all be reworked into your outfits with a little imagination. Would you wear an eight-inch diamante stone on your head or around your waist? Think small all the time.

You can also use children's cheap gilt jewelry. A ring becomes a bracelet, tiny charms become earrings. Make your own appliqué trims by embroidering motifs either by hand or on your machine. Bond them to a backing fabric before cutting them out and apply to the garment once awkward seams and darts are complete.

There's also a great wealth of ready-made motifs that could be incorporated onto your doll clothes with the minimum of fuss and effort. Look out for vintage 50's hats, which can be taken apart and will give you netting, feathers, velvet, silk flowers and even wire to reuse. Feathers can also be bought by the package in craft stores or from angling supply stores. Watch for the sparkly chenille braid sold in such establishments which is used for fly making by fishermen, as it's much cheaper than regular embroidery packages. Your local dressmaking store will sell feather by the meter/yard i.e. marabou trim

If using old mink trim, pop it into a freezer bag and leave in the freezer for a few days. Then give it a good shake before using. Cut mink on the wrong side with a craft knife to avoid spoiling the fur itself. Apply onto fabric using a rubber glue compound.

Egg-crafting supply companies sell wonderful filigree metal findings or charms that can be applied to clothes. They also carry poly-glitter, which can be added to appliqués with fabric glue, and a wide range of miniature trims and braids. Look for old millinery supplies, as the old pressed velvet flowers make wonderful doll hats simply used on their own. Sugar-crafting supplies yield yet more trinkets and trims—stamens for hats, charms for jewelry, and green wire flower stems that are great for flowers on hats or curly vine effects if so desired.

Miniature dollhouse or teddy bear suppliers sell wonderful scaled down items usually 1/12 or 1/10 scale, which can, if carefully picked, be utilized for your dolls. A few websites now provide Play scale paper ephemera that can be printed out and used as accessories with outfits i.e. newspapers, playing cards, boxes, passports, greetings cards, invitations.

FASHION & COSTUME REFERENCE BOOKS:

Some may be out of print (OOP) but are worth searching for in libraries and in vintage and second-hand bookstores.

These five books, all by John Peacock published by Thames and Hudson, are wonderfully inexpensive and packed with informative ideas.

Fashion Sourcebooks: The 1920's
Fashion Sourcebooks: The 1930's
Fashion Sourcebooks: The 1940's
Fashion Sourcebooks: The 1950's
Fashion Sourcebooks: The 1960's
Fashion Sourcebooks: The 1970's
Fashion in the Thirties and *Fashion in the Forties* by Julian Robinson published by St. Martin's Press Inc. (OOP)
The Golden Age of Style: Art Deco Fashion Illustration by Julian Robinson published by Harcourt Brace Jovanovich
In Vogue: Six Decades of Fashion by Georgina Howell
Costume and Fashion: A Concise History by James Laver published by Thames and Hudson: World of Art Series

In A Glamorous Fashion: The Fabulous Years of Hollywood Costume Design by W. Robert La Vine published by George Allen & Unwin 1981 (OOP)

Glamour In Fashion by David Bond published by Guinness Pub., Ltd

Fashions of the Roaring Twenties by Laurie Laubner published by Schiffer

Forties Fashion and the New Look by Colin McDowell published by Bloomsbury

The Collectors Book of Twentieth-Century Fashion by Frances Kennett published byGranada (OOP)

Let There Be Clothes: 4,000 Years of Fashion (fashion trivia) by Lyn Schnurnberger published by Workman Publishing, NY.

Vintage Hats & Bonnets 1770–1970 by Susan Langley published by Schroeder Pub & Co.

Costume Design in the Movies by Elizabeth Leese published by Dover

Fashion in Film by Regine and P.W. Engelmeier published by Prestel

Hollywood and History: Costume Design in Film by LA County Museum of Art published by Thames and Hudson

INTERNET COSTUME SITES:

http://www.marquise.de/
La Couturiere Parisienne Costume and Fashion Site

http://www.costumes.org/
The Costumer's Manifesto

http://milieux.com/costume/
Milieux: The Costume Site

http://locutus.ucr.edu/~cathy/rd.html
The Regency Fashion Page

http://www.louisville.edu/~kprayb01/1920s.html
The 1920's a site dedicated to the Roaring 20's

http://members.tripod.com/slowdyve/
GLAMOUR_CENTRAL.html
Glamour Central- Retro Culture

http://www.fortunecity.com/lavender/heat/218/
Celluloid Wrappers: Costume in the Movies

http://www.geocities.com/FashionAvenue/5362/
1966 History of Mod Fashion

http://www.firstview.com/designerlist/index.html
Contemporary Designers Fashion Collections

http://www.fashionlive.com/
The best in current styles and trends with revolving fashion plates

INTERNET SEWING/EMBROIDERY RESOURCES:

http://www.lacis.com/
Resource for ribbons, threads, silk and velvet flowers for textile arts

http://www.minidolls.com/home.shtml
Miniature doll making supplies

http://www.vintagevogue.com/html/our_company.shtml
Ribbons and trims

http://www.french-treasures.com/
French Treasures (vintage cloth from 18th /early 20th C.'s)

http://www.vintagecat.com/fashion.htm
Source for vintage magazines, patterns and books

http://www.ccartwright.com/index.html
Source for miniature beads and sequins

http://flightsoffancyboutique.com/
Beaded fringe, vintage blossoms and leaves, trims

http://www.rosecottage.com
Vintage millinery supplies trims, and textiles
Rose Cottage
363 Main Street
Thomaston, Maine 04861USA

http://member.aol.com/hofhcat/jharcat.htm
Fashion doll supplies
House of Harcat
2354 Aqua Vista Avenue
Henderson, Nevada 89014 USA
Email: jharcat@aol.com
Tel: 702 456-0659

http://www.quiltware.com
Embellishments, charms, flower appliqués, lace doilies
3 Crabapple Court
Mullica Hill, NJ 08062
Email: quiltware@mindspring.com
Tel:1-888-734-1964
Fax: 303-374-7981

http://www.karimeaway.com/
Tiny mother if pearl buttons, charms
Email: karimeaway@aol.com
Tel:714-921-9184

http://www.printmini.com
Wonderful printable paper accessories for Fashion Dolls i.e. newspapers, playing cards, money, passports, also templates for making hat & candy boxes, shopping carriers etc..

JEWELRY USED IN BOOK:

Much of the fine pieces of costume jewelry worn by the dolls in this book were provided by:
Kim Fisher of The Finishing Touch
Email: finishingtouch@inficad.com
www.inficad.com/~finishingtouch/
Isabel & Fernando Betancourt of Bijoux Fantasie
www.betancourtandcompany.com

MAIL ORDER/SHOP ADDRESSES:

www.thewalters.com
Porcelain Shoe Kits for Fashion dolls
Email: schnaushe@yahoo.com
Sally Walters
4760 Fox Creek Road
Carson City, NV 89703
Tel/Fax: 775-883-584
Mini-Magic
3910 Patricia Drive
Columbus, OH 43220
Tel: 614/457-3687
Doll and small scale supplies
Au Fils Du Temps
64 Bis Rue Du Dr. Peltier
B.P. 56
17302 Rochefort Cedex
France
(Wonderful selection of Vintage French Fashion and Costume magazines, viewed by appointment only)
Email: ryphat.aft@wanadoo.fr

General Instructions

OUTFITS

All the outfits in this book fit 15"/16" dolls i.e. Gene®, Tyler®, Esme®, FM vinyl dolls etc. ALL pieces will have to be enlarged using a photocopier at 135%. Some patterns need to be pieced together at certain places because of their size, and some are labeled *NOT TO SCALE*. Patterns labeled in this manner must be drawn according to the measurements given on the piece. They are typically simple rectangles and do not involve complicated shapes.

STAR RATINGS

The patterns have been star rated to show the standard of sewing skills required.

* indicates that the pattern is very simple to sew for a beginner or a sewer with average skill.

** indicates the pattern is suitable for an average sewer or the slightly more adventurous.

*** indicates that the pattern is somewhat more complicated and is for an experienced sewer.

SEWING TIPS
FABRICS—COLOUR ,TEXTURE, WEIGHT:

When possible, use natural fabrics for doll clothes i.e. silk, cotton, lawn, silk satin, taffeta, fine woolen crepes and tweeds, and cotton laces.

Scale is of the utmost importance when choosing patterns on fabric or laces. Remember each period had it's own styles in fabrics and colours, so try to be sympathetic to your chosen design, and research your outfit through old magazines, costume books and period films.

Choose the finest or lightest weights in all fabrics so that it will hang and drape properly. The same goes for linings. These must be sympathetic to your main fabric, and should not add bulk or act like a cardboard stiffener unless you want that look say in a collar, hat, or corset. Instead of using heavy velvet consider using knit back velvet or velour, which takes darts, and tiny seams without adding bulk.

The correct combination of all three can make or break your outfit. Don't be afraid to experiment with colour combinations. Be daring, and if you don't feel you have the confidence to experiment, make a scrapbook of photos of nature, cut up magazines, and fashion photos from which you can borrow when you need inspiration.

PATTERNS:

Photocopy all patterns in this book enlarging them to 135%. Because many pieces were too large for the pages of the book, the patterns were reduced and will not fit your doll at their current size. Some patterns must be pieced together because of their size, and others are labeled *NOT TO SCALE* and must be redrawn using the measurements given on the piece. Such pieces are typically simple rectangles and do not involve complicated shapes. To avoid pin-marking or thread pulling on fine fabrics, draw around patterns straight onto fabric with tailor's chalk or air-soluble pen.

Mark dart, braid, trim or bead placement lines and notches on the fabric with dressmaker's carbon paper or very lightly with hard lead pencil .

The seam allowance, which is included on the pattern pieces, is 1/4in (0.5cm), which is narrow but will reduce the bulk when pressing. Use Fray-Check® where appropriate around sleeve or neck seams or where a certain amount of stress or stretching of the fabric may occur. Some stay stitching will also be necessary to reinforce some seams i.e. at curves or fabric cut on bias.

One point to remember when taking measurements for long or full skirts, if you wish to adapt a pattern in this book, measure the doll from waist to floor with doll securely on her stand! If you don't, your skirt will flap like a pelmet around her shoes with an unsightly stand showing underneath. Allow at least and extra 1cm or half inch plus allowance for hem.

STITCHING:

All the outfits shown in this book have been made using a sewing machine, but they could just as easily be hand-stitched. Most hems are turned twice, not overlocked (serged) as this bulk will show when pressing. This is purely a personal choice. If you own an overlocker, you are more than welcome to use it, but for fine silks, I think hand finishing is the best method. A loose zig-zag stitch on your machine is a good alternative for finishing raw edges. In addition, use a fine needle and a shorter stitch length for seams, lengthening stitches for curves for flexibility. If you wish to make up garments using French seams, especially on sheer fabrics, remember to allow a wider seam allowance when cutting.

PRESSING:

Press each seam immediately after sewing for a better finish! A small traveling iron and a sleeve board make pressing easier, as does a damp cotton cloth instead of spray steam, which might soak the entire garment instead of just isolated segments. For those inaccessible places such as the shoulder seams, a padded "ham" can be made using basically two ovals of cloth sewn together then softly stuffed with wadding. This can be easily molded and then inserted into the area to be ironed. You could also cover little ironing board shapes cut from thick balsa wood covered with a few layers of felt, which again, can be inserted into small areas.

FASTENINGS:

Small buttonholes can be made by hand, but are difficult to finish neatly unless your stitches are neat and tidy. You may find it easier to sew small loops to fasten buttons. Hooks must be securely sewn on. Snaps can be bought in black and steel finishes in tiny sizes (00 and 000) as well as clear plastic, which are useful when using fine fabrics as they blend into the fabric and are less bulky. Miniature zippers can also be used if desired, but again, are tricky to install and can add extra bulk to finished or curved areas.

ACCESSORIES:

These complete an outfit. Each period was defined by the style of the day, which included accessories. Each outfit has it's own accessories with some of the same techniques being carried over from pattern to pattern. So in some instances the directions for such items will be given only once—gloves or stockings for example.

SEWING NOTIONS:

Bondaweb®
Brown paper, tracing paper/baking parchment, lightweight card
Buckram
Dressmakers cutting scissors
Dressmakers pins (I recommend Bridal pins as they are very long and fine)
Embroiderers scissors
Embroidery hoops
Fray-check®
Paper scissors
Plastic coated wire (as found securing toys in toy boxes)
Press studs/hooks and eye's/zips (as discussed)
Safety pins
Seam ripper
Selection of interlining and facings
Selection of needles, including long fine beading needles
Tailors chalk or soluble pen
Tape measure

SEAMS AND STITCHES

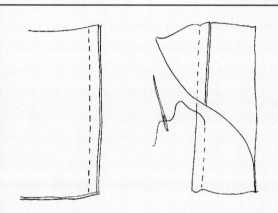

A French Seam:
Unlike most construction seams, the fabric is joined with wrong sides together. Turn the seam; press, and sew next seam next to the inner seam allowance, enclosing it neatly. This seam is useful for finishing chiffon or sheer overskirts in particular.

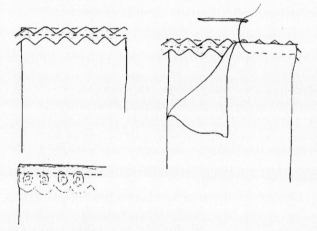

Inserting trim, ribbon or lace into seams:
Make your seams on jackets, necklines, etc. more interesting with contrasting trim by stitching it in place before closing seam with opposing fabric.

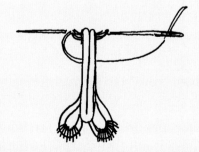

Sewing on a hook may seen straightforward, however, if you distribute the stitches around the hook, it also distributes the strain on the hook thus producing a neater closure without unsightly gaps.

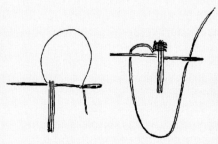

Worked bars and loops give a more professional finish to your garment and they look better especially if the bar is to the front. However if there is a lot of strain to be put upon the closure, i.e. on a corset back, a metal bar is more suitable. Work a few small straight stitches in desired position. Then work buttonhole stitches down the bar until straight stitches are completely covered. Loops can be formed on edges in this way too, and covered with buttonhole stitches. This gives a lovely finish to an edge especially if you have tiny buttons or beads as fastenings.

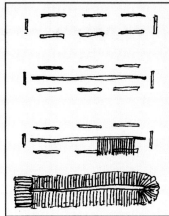

A simple buttonhole should be worked at the smallest scale you can—ideally 1/4 in (4mm). It looks great, but you have to have patience to complete this task!

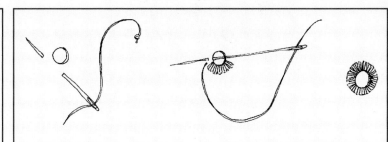

An eyelet worked into fabric can substitute for a buttonhole, but your fabric must be robust or you will end up with a frayed messy hole. Make hole with a blunt darning needle and work buttonhole stitch around edges. Work as close as you can. This looks wonderful when worked in gold or silver thread with pearl bead buttons.

Simple running stitch used for tacking down edges etc.

Hem stitch; best used to fasten down hems on fine or sheer fabrics.

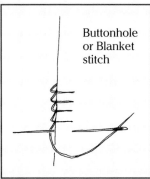

Buttonhole or Blanket stitch

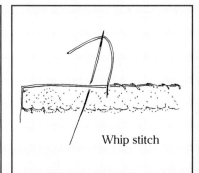

Whip stitch

Blind Stitch; best used on seams that will be visible to outer part of garment if hand finishing is essential.

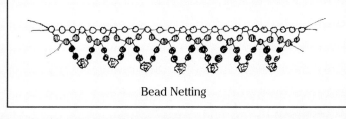

Bead Netting

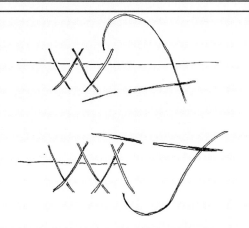

Cross hem stitch; a robust form of hemming that can be used on heavier weights of fabrics.

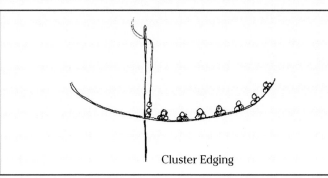

Cluster Edging

Back stitch; this stitch can be used to stitch seams where a machine cannot go. For instance, this works well in a particularly small sleeve insertion or for stitching bags and purses. With care, you can work this stitch to tiny proportions, and will find it's just as strong as any machined seam when complete.

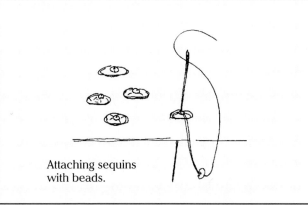

Attaching sequins with beads.

Late Victorian Costume c. 1875-1880

Illustration 1. Too Early, painting by Tissot, 1873.

Towards the end of the 19th Century, the bustle (that predominant bump at a ladies posterior) began to disappear. Skirts became narrower. Long fan-shaped trains that were sometimes detachable were popular, and draped fabrics and bows took the bustles place at the rear, literally. Deep pleats controlled any fullness at the waist. Waists were ferociously tight-laced by wearing corsets outside, as part of the bodice, running to a sharp point at the front. The skirt was horizontally draped with lace to emphasize the waist and make it look smaller still. A specific mode of dress for the upper classes was strictly adhered to especially for certain occasions such as those attended by Royalty. Low décolletages and short sleeves were compulsory, long gloves essential, and a tiara or hair decoration compulsory. When researching nineteenth-century costume, no painter can be more useful to the costume historian than James Tissot. He observed toilettes of the period with the greatest attention to detail and painted them with meticulous accuracy, recording that era's choice of colour and style.

Illustration 2. Evening
Dresses, c. 1877. *Costume
& Fashion* by James Laver.

Illustration 3. Royal Museum
of Scotland Cream Court
Dress. Picture card No. 4,
c. 1887.

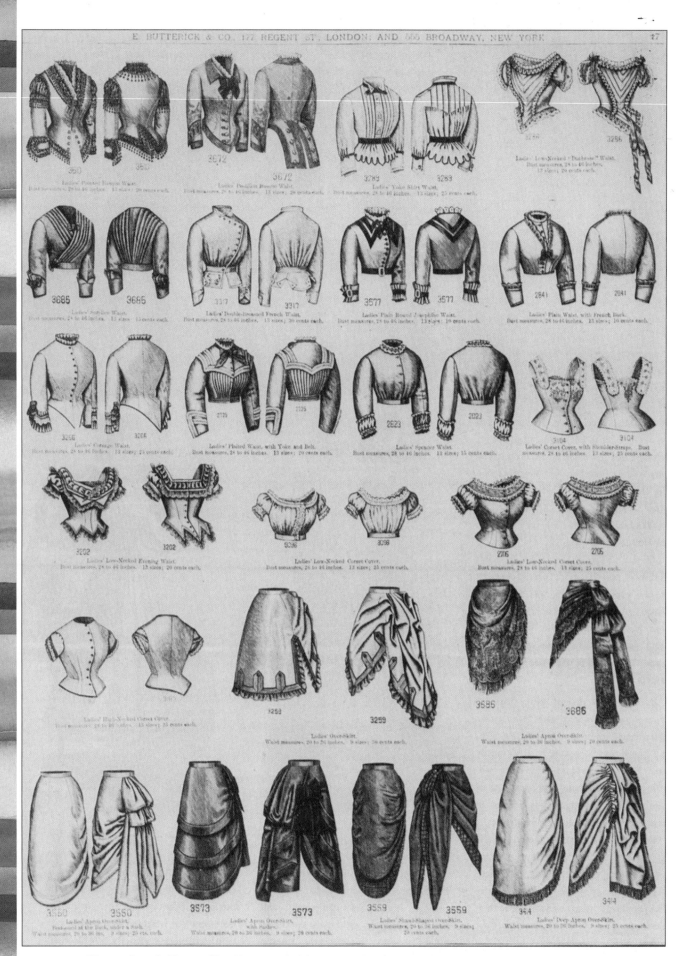

Illustration 4. Chart of bodices and skirts. Late 1800s. *Butterick Fashions,* Autumn 1915.

Star Rating ***
Modeled by a Stardust Memories Gene® doll.
Jewelry by Kim Fisher of The Finishing Touch

Illustration 5

Attending the Opera, especially during the Season, was a serious affair. Everyone who was anyone would be there so it was important to be seen at one's best. You would definitely be wearing your most precious jewels and probably a new gown and cloak by the famous couturier, Monsieur Worth, a favorite of Royalty, Aristocracy, and those known snobbishly as "the New Money."

I've chosen an off-white satin brocade as my main fabric, a claret velvet for the cloak, and found a claret velvet ribbon to match for the trimmings. I also found ribbon roses braid which came in claret and cream. Pearls, beads and micro beads were chosen to compliment and contrast with these fabrics.

Pattern Pieces:
V1 Cape
V2 Skirt Front
V3 Corset
V4 Side & Back Skirt
V5 Lace Front Drape
V6 Lace Train

For pattern pieces see pages 113-117

Materials:

½ yard/meter of satin brocade or similar
½ yard/meter of lace
  (choose lace with one finished edge)
¼ yard/meter of fine weight velvet
1 yard/meter of ribbon rose braid
¼ yard/meter contrasting colour of same ribbon
  rose braid
½ yard/meter of velvet ribbon (same colour as
  velvet) that is 1/4in (1cm) in width
7in/18cm satin ribbon that is 1in (2.5cm) in width
4in/10cm open work lace for collar
heavy interfacing
small lace doily or crochet mat
off-white nylon or Lycra for gloves

selection of small pearl, seed and micro beads
fuse and florist or milliners fine gilt wire
embroiderers gold purl wire (very fine miniature
  coiled spring which can be pulled open)
small spray of vintage flowers or buds
pack of 2mm silk ribbon
small piece of organza ribbon for fan
gilt filigree for fan
metallic card for backing
three feathers
hooks and eyes
bull-dog clips
pliers for cutting wire
thread to match

13

Illustration 6

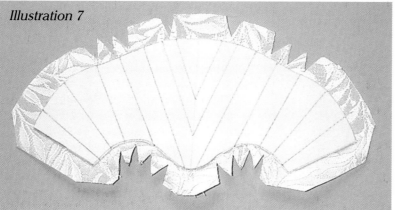

Illustration 7

Illustration 8

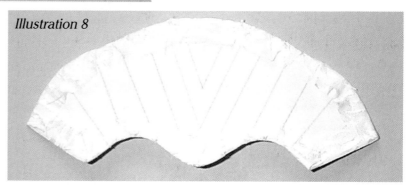

Corset: V3 Corset *(Illustration 6)*

1. Prepare fabrics by ironing out any creases. Cut a rectangle of stiff interfacing 7in x 4in (18 cm x 10cm). Then cut Bondaweb® or fusing material slightly smaller than this. Draw corset shape and stitching lines onto interfacing. Then iron fusible fabric to other side.

2. Cut out corset shape and peel off backing paper. Then iron the corset onto wrong side of brocade fabric

3. Cut around corset leaving ¾in (1.5cm) allowance. At curved points cut notches into allowance, but do not go right up to interfacing—leave at least 1/16in (1mm) to prevent fraying. *Illustration 7.*

4. Turn raw edges over carefully folding and tacking as you go around curves to create a smooth edge. *Illustration 8.*

5. Pin corset to wrong side of the lining fabric and trim to shape. Sandwich the raw edges around entire corset edge between lining and interfacing with tiny slip stitches. Cut notches at curves. Take care to miter corners and trim excess fabric so there is no unsightly bulk that affects the fit on the doll. *Illustration 9.*

6. Fit corset to doll and mark closure points for metal hook and eye closures.

7. For straps, stitch contrasting ribbon trim onto velvet ribbon. Mark and cut required lengths by placing corset on doll and pinning straps in place. Cut and sew to inside of corset. Cut another length to fit between straps at bodice front. Cut and stitch neatly into place.

8. Finish off all threads securely to inside of corset. *Illustration 10.*

9. Attach three rows of pearls to front and back of strap to straddle upper arm. It's best to do this while the doll is wearing the corset for perfect fit and so both sides hang in balance. Also, individual pearls can be sewn in the centers of each ribbon rose for a decorative effect. *Illustration 11.*

14

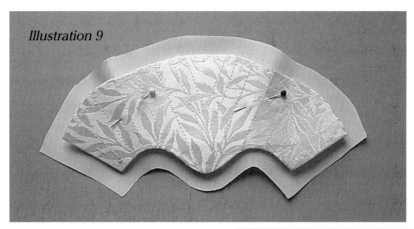

Illustration 9

Illustration 10

Illustration 11

15

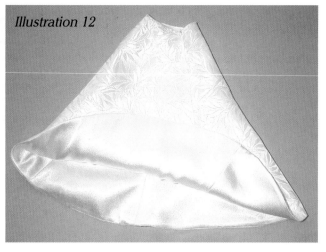

Illustration 12

Illustration 13

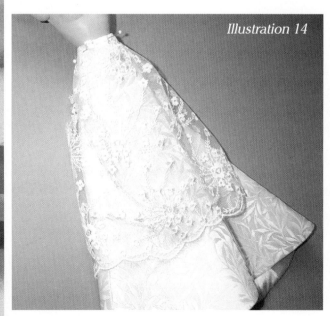

Illustration 14

Skirt:
V2 Skirt Front, V4 Side & Back Skirt, V5 Lace Front Drape, V6 Lace Train

1. Cut and join the front and the two side back sections. Press seams flat turning edges for center back opening

2. Cut and stitch lining. Then with right sides together, pin and stitch around entire hemline. Turn work to right side and press flat. *Illustration 12.*

3. Turn raw edges of waistline to inside and slip stitch together. Put skirt on doll and fit waistline by pinning waist shut and sewing on a press stud. Then fold two tucks away from center back towards side. Stitch in place at waistline. This produces a pleated train effect falling from waist at sides. *Illustration 13.*

4. Cut front lace drape with finished edge to bottom. Stitch in gathering threads, but do not pull up at this point. Put skirt on doll and pin drape to skirt. Between tucks at side, gather fullness around waist working from center front towards each side folding in tucks. Stitch in place using tiny stab stitches into main brocade fabric. Pull vertical gathering threads to shape front drape, longer at front, shorter to sides. Secure in place again with tiny stab stitches. Take off doll and press in place, catching any loosed bulk with tiny stitches. *Illustrations 14 and 15.*

Illustration 15

Illustration 16

5. Cut out lace train and stitch in gathering threads at points shown on pattern. Pull into required width as indicated. Cut a length of 1in (2.5cm) satin ribbon to fit across top of train. Pin to top edge of train and sew in place. Machine stitch two gathering rows at top and base of ribbon and pull in fitting across back of skirt, between skirt side tucks, and meeting edges of skirt drape. *Illustration 16.*

6. Secure thread gathers and finish ribbon edges to inside. Press flat. Stitch one edge of ribbon to one side of drape, sewing a hook and eye closure at other side. This will cover back opening on brocade skirt. *Illustration 17.*

7. Using the ribbon rose trim, pin around entire train edge covering raw edges. Also, pin over gathering threads at two gathered sections. Sew in place with small back stitches or machine in place using a zipper foot (the bulky parts of the trim might get stuck in-between the legs of a regular presser foot). Individual pearls can then be stitched into the centers of these roses. *Illustration 18.*

Illustration 18

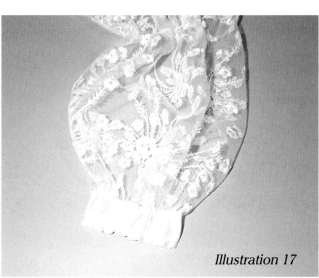

Illustration 17

17

Illustration 19

Opera Cape: V1 Cape
Illustrations 19 and 20

1. Cut out velvet and contrasting lining. Stitch shoulder darts. Then with right sides together, stitch around entire outer edge leaving small opening in the bottom center back for turning. Turn inside out and press flat (using velvet board or fluffy towel to avoid marking velvet)

2. Cut to the center of your lace doily for neck opening. Ease and pin in place around neck edge and down center front.

3. Take 4in (10cm) of open work lace for collar. Thread a piece of velvet ribbon through base. Pull to fit around neck edge. Cut ribbon and lace and finish off raw edges by turning to inside and overstitching to prevent fraying. *Illustration 21.*

4. Pin lace/velvet collar to neck edge and slip stitch in place on inside of work. Add small pieces of rose trim down each side of center front to where doily ends. *Illustration 22.*

5. Add hook and eye closure, working a thread loop instead of using a metal bar. *Illustration 23.*

Illustration 20

18

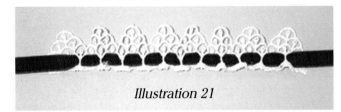

Illustration 21

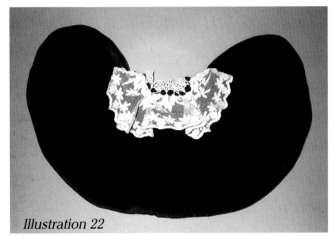

Illustration 22

Illustration 23

Illustration 24

Feathered Fan
1. Cut foil card to match filigree by tracing around it and cutting with a craft knife. Sparingly cover the card with glue and carefully place three feathers onto it. Brush glue onto wrong side of filigree and press on top of feathers wiping off any excess that squeezes through.
2. Use heavy-duty bull dog clips to hold in place while the glue dries. Add organza ribbon handle to base. *Illustration 24.*

Gloves
Use the opera length glove pattern, and off white Lycra or nylon material. Follow instructions for gloves as given in *Forties Fashions* chapter.

Illustration 25

Decorative Floral Headpiece
Illustration 25

1. Using gilt or fuse wire at least 6in (15cm) in length, make various beaded floral shapes and leaves. *Illustration 26.*

2. Gradually layer and bind flower stamens together with fine fuse wire or thread, taking care to alternate contrasting shapes and colours. Once you've finished your layering, wind 2mm silk ribbon around wire or thread to hide stems finishing with a couple of tiny bows at base. A small dab of glue may be needed here to keep bows in required position. *Illustration 27.*

3. Use large pearl-headed pins to keep hairpiece in position on dolls head. The decorative headpiece can be pulled into desired shape using the doll's hairstyle as a guide. *Illustration 28.*

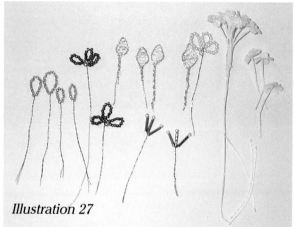

Illustration 27

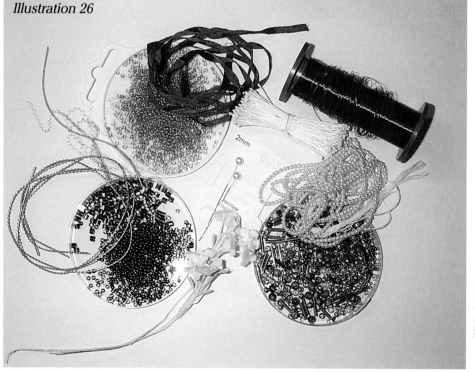

Illustration 26

Illustration 28

Edwardian 'S'-Shaped Dress c. 1900-1905

The Edwardian era in England is generally thought of as those years from the beginning of the century to the outbreak of World War I, whereas in France, the period was known as La Belle Epoque. The King favored mature women with womanly figures, so fashion followed suite. This produced the characteristic S-Line—the bust thrust forward, accentuated by frills and flounces, the abdomen thrown backwards. Known as "trumpet" skirts, they were tightly smoothed over hips with the plentiful gored panels flaring out in the shape of a bell towards the ground. Lace, if not real lace, then Irish crochet, was abundant. During the day, the figure was covered from chin to toe with frills and flounces, but by night, extravagantly decorated décolletage's was de rigueur. Hair was piled high on the head, and even larger hats were balanced precariously on top. Fashionable ladies such as Sarah Bernhardt and Lily Langtry, stars of the theatre, were a great influence on fashion. Indeed, clothes were so richly decorated and embellished they made the women look like elaborate theatrical fantasies in themselves.

Illustration 31. Evening gown of line brussels net, worked with ribbon embroidery, in Pompador, Penelope Crepe Edge, and empire ribbon. *Needlecraft.*

Above:
Illustration 29. Evening dress, c. 1901. *Costume & Fashion* by James Laver.

Illustration 30. Chiffon dress, c. 1901. *Costume & Fashion* by James Laver.

Illustration 32. Summer dress, c. 1903. *Costume & Fashion* by James Laver.

Illustration 33. Silk evening dress, c. 1911. *Costume & Fashion* by James Laver.

BY SPECIAL APPOINTMENT

HATTERS TO THE ROYAL FAMILY.

AUTUMN FASHIONS

NEW ILLUSTRATED CATALOGUE

ON APPLICATION POST FREE.

A choice selection sent on approval on receipt of Trade reference.

No. 1 L.—*A PICTURE HAT* in silk and velvet, with slightly mushroom brim, and a softly draped crown which finishes in the front with a knot of velvet and an ostrich plume.

No. 3 L.—*A USEFUL FELT HAT* with a becoming rounded curve to the edge of brim. Smartly trimmed with a puffed silk feather in shaded effects.

No. 13 L.—*A DRESSY TOQUE* in silk beaver, with a trimming of ribbon encircling the folds on the crown; the plumage tips on the bandeau give a very soft effect to the left side. This can be made in all the newest shades.

SCOTTS
1 OLD BOND STREET W

Illustration 34. Hat advertisement. *Needlecraft.*

Star Rating ***
Modeled by Dream Girl Gene®, 1998 Hollywood Convention Doll
Jewelry: single Wedgwood earring as brooch; pearl studs are model's own.

Illustration 35

A charming spring silhouette for walking in the park, complete with satiny parasol—a must for any Edwardian lady's wardrobe. A typical high-necked waist is attached to a trumpet skirt, cinched tightly in by a brocade girdle. The skirt festooned with layers of laces, tucks and bows. Every curve of the wearer's figure was hinted at. The embodiment of this ideal was indeed drawn by the American illustrator, Charles Dana Gibson and became known as the Gibson Girl.

Pattern Pieces:
EG1 Bodice Front
EG2 Bodice Back
EG3 Upper Sleeve
EG4 Lower Sleeve
EG5 Collar
EG6 Girdle
EG7 Skirt Front
EG8 Sides
EG9 Back
EG10 Parasol

For pattern pieces
see pages 118-121

Materials:
1yard/meter fine polyester silk or satin (or pure silk)
¾ yard/meter sateen brocade
12in (31cm) square of vintage lace, or chiffon, old hanky etc.
selection of lace trims, in a variety of widths, vintage or otherwise
small buttons or pearls
miniature straw boater hat (which you've painted with pearlized acrylic paint)
silk or velvet flowers to trim hat
½ yard/meter of wired ribbon
10in (25cm) wooden skewer (which you've painted and varnished if desired)
large glass bead
long conical fancy filigree shape

Illustration 36

Dress
See Illustration 36

1. Gather a selection of colour coordinated satins, brocades, and vintage trims and laces. If you do not have access to these, cotton laces can be immersed in tea, left for a few hours, rinsed and pressed, and you have your own vintage lace! *Illustration 37.*

2. Place bodice front pattern onto vintage fabric, or material of your choice choosing area carefully if tucks or lace is involved. Cut out satin bodice front, and stitch two fronts together as one. Treat then as single piece. *Illustration 38.*

3. Do the same for lower sleeves, selecting area of vintage fabric carefully. Cut then stitch to satin lower sleeve. *Illustration 39.*

4. Stitch cuff edge of lower sleeve to lining. Turn in closure edge between points, and slipstitch or machine in place.

Illustration 37

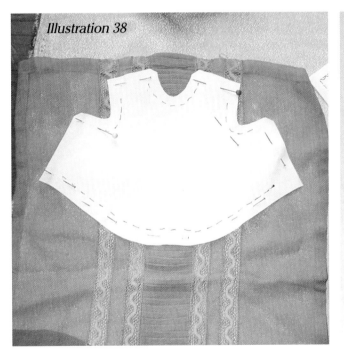

Illustration 38

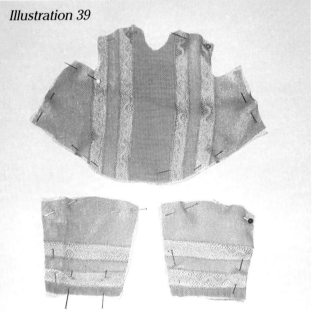

Illustration 39

5. Gather lower edge of upper sleeve to fit top edge of lower sleeve, and stitch in place. Turn back lower cuff edges and slip stitch in place. *Illustration 40.*

6. Sew backs onto bodice front at shoulders. Then set in sleeves, gathering in fullness between dots and easing sleeves into armholes. *Illustration 41.*

7. Sew the front, sides and back sides of the skirt together. Do not sew center back seam. Press all seams flat. Take your variety of trims and place them on skirt, trying them in different positions, layering one over another, before finally sewing them into position. Make sure they will match when center back seam is sewn. *Illustration 42.*

8. Attach satin collar to neck edge. Turn in half and slipstitch edges in place. *See Illustration 43.*

9. Add lace trim to collar if desired at this point. *Illustration 44.*

10. Try bodice on doll and fold in center back seams. Mark closure points and sew on snaps. Adjust front bodice gathers at lower edge. Note that the front should blouse out quite a bit. This shape is enhanced by the girdle, which cinched in the waist forming the popular Edwardian S-Line.

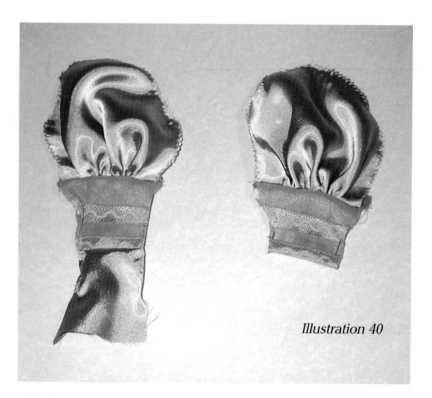

Illustration 40

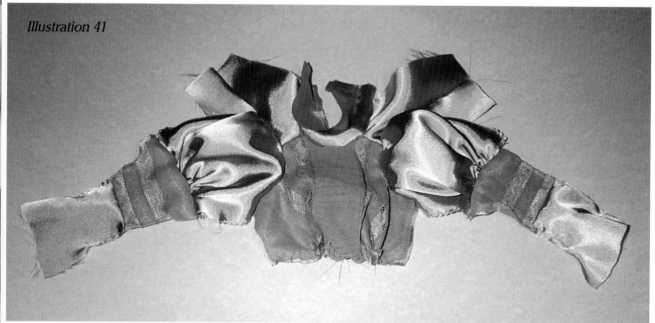

Illustration 41

26

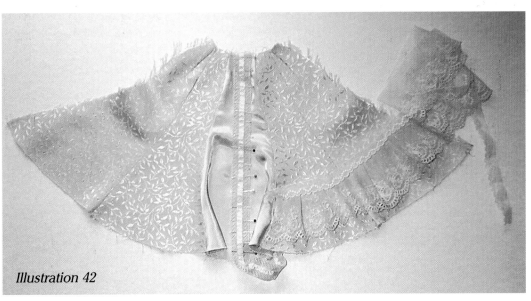

Illustration 42

Illustration 43

Illustration 44

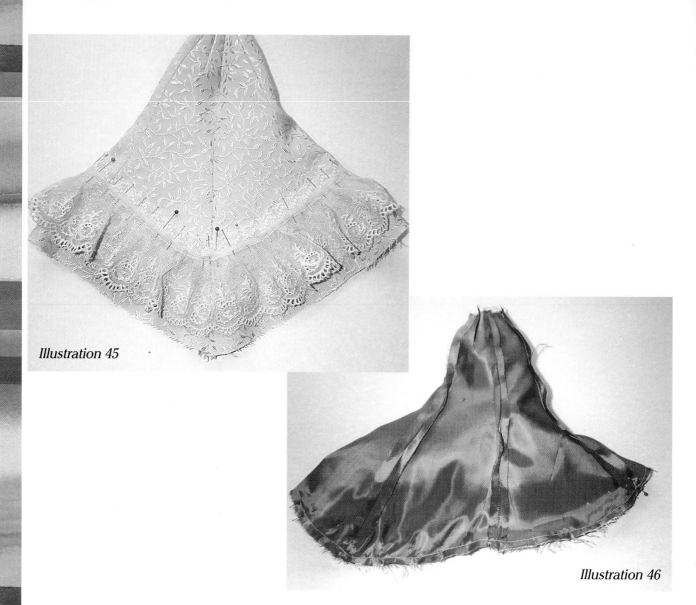

Illustration 45

Illustration 46

11. Make sure you match lace edgings on skirt at back. Stitch on any smaller laces to hide previous gathering or stitching lines before you stitch on the lining to hem. *Illustration 45.*

12. Stitch lining together as main skirt. With right sides together, ensuring all lace trims are pinned up out of the way, stitch lining and main fabric together around entire hemline. *Illustration 46.*

13. Turn lining to inside and press hemline. Pin bodice to right sides of skirt and stitch in place, gathering front to fit waistline. Turn ½in (1.5cm) on lining waistline and sandwich main skirt and bodice raw edges under turning. Slipstitch in place. Add snap closure to skirt back. *Illustration 47.*

Illustration 47

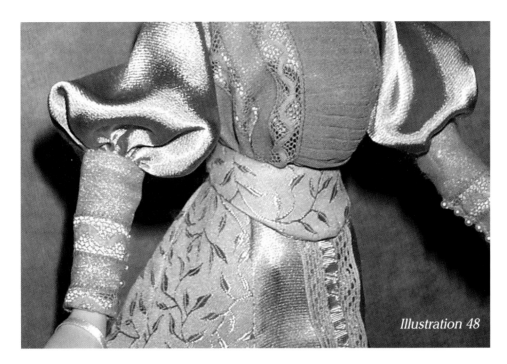

Illustration 48

Illustration 49

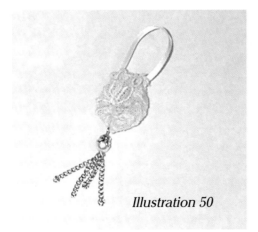

Illustration 50

Girdle:
EG6 Girdle
Illustration 48

Cut and sew main fabric and lining girdle pieces together leaving opening at top edge for turning. Turn inside out and press, finishing open edge. Try on doll over skirt and mark closure points. Sew on hooks and eyes.

Hat
Illustration 49

Paint your straw boater with your choice of acrylic paint to match or contrast with outfit. You do not need to varnish it. Pin loosely and arrange wired ribbon around brim. Then stitch or glue in place around side of crown with hot glue gun. Stick or sew on flowers, interspersed with stamens and leaves, around brim hiding join in ribbon. Add bow at the back and use large pearl-headed pins to secure to doll's hair.

Bag
Illustration 50

Cut 1-½in (4cm) of lace and join each edge. Gather bottom and pull tight. Then fasten off. Sew a length of 2mm silk ribbon for handle to each side of top. Run a row of gathering stitches along top and gather loosely, stuffing inside with tiny piece of waste satin material. Then pull thread and close. Add a beaded tassel to bottom of bag.

29

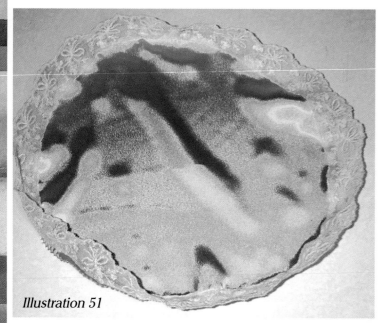

Illustration 51

Parasol

1. Cut circle of satin or lace using pattern and finish raw edges. Pin a length of lace or trim to edge of right side of fabric. *Illustration 51.*

2. Marking center point, make a tiny hole in circle of fabric. Push the wooden skewer through to wrong side so that approximately ½in (1cm) shows through. Then brush bottom of skewer with glue. *Illustration 52.*

3. Gather up circle of fabric around skewer and tie in place with a length or ribbon. Glue large glass bead to top of skewer and wrap some ribbon under this leaving some loose to tie into a handle for securing to dolls wrist. After dabbing with glue, push bottom of skewer into conical filigree wiping off any glue that seeps through. *Illustration 53.*

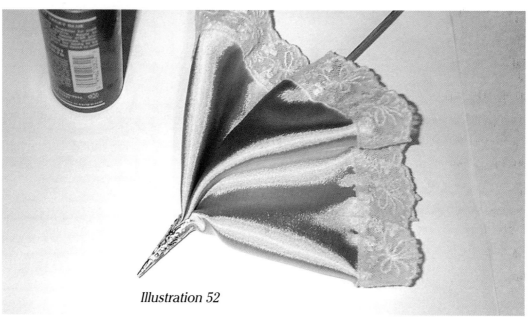

Illustration 52

Illustration 53

Twenties Flapper Dress and Cloche Hat
c. 1927

The 1920's were the first decade not to look to Paris for inspiration. Women and men now had their fantasies played out on the Silver Screen. Hollywood stars such as Pola Negri, Gloria Swanson, Louise Brooks, and the "IT" girl, Clara Bow, captivated women. New ideals of unreal splendor and romantic beauty were established. Gone were the soft muted colours of the Edwardian era as well as the curvaceous S-Line. This was to be replaced with flat-chested, bobbed, shingle-headed girls dressed in bright geometric tubular "flapper" or "garconne" short dresses. Towards the end of the decade, many couturiers tried to lengthen the skirts by means of flounces, transparent and asymmetrical hemlines, side-pieces and trains, but women still embraced this new-found "emancipation." Designers such as Schiaparelli used these flat canvases for abstract and surreal images and wonderful embellishment.

Above: Illustration 54. La Mode French magazine. Janvier, 1927.

Left: Illustration 55. Page from an unidentified French magazine with four short chiffon evening dresses.

31

Star Rating *

Modeled by restyled, re-painted Breathless and Pin Up dolls
Jewelry by Kim Fisher of The Finishing Touch

Illustration 56

Illustration 57

Illustration 58

Two Flapper's raring to go dance the Charleston at a popular Jazz club, or maybe Tango the night away in a dark Speakeasy Club. They may wear fashionable, boyishly straight dresses, but there's nothing androgynous about these girls with their smoldering eyes, playing the Vamp. They're out to get their man!

This is a very easy pattern to make up, and the possibilities are endless for embellishing the body of the dress. With a little thought and imagination, you can transform this simplest of styles into something quite elaborate. Or you can keep it as simple as you like by using wonderful fabric. Look to vintage garments here as the embroidered front of a blouse or the beaded yoke of a dress could give you just the fabric you need to make this dress.

Illustration 59

Pattern Pieces:
Dress
TW1 Dress
TW2 Hanky Flounce
Cloche Hat
TWC1 Front
TWC2 Back
TWC3 Sides

For pattern pieces see pages 122-123

Materials:
Cloche Hat
small 6in (15cm) square piece of velvet, felt, or chosen main fabric
lining, if required, to match
various trims, braid, feathers, beads, flowers, appliqué shapes
Dress
piece of fabric 14in x 14in (36cm x 36cm) (I used vintage chiffon hankies)
coordinating satin for lining
beaded fringing
feathers
filigree fan shape or tie pin front
ribbon, braid or lace to trim
beads and/or pearls, diamante, glass stones
press studs
marabou trim, 12in (31cm) approx

Illustration 60

Illustration 61

Illustration 62

Illustration 63

34

Dress:
TW1 Dress, TW2 Hanky Flounce
Illustrations 61, 62 and 63

1. Find a piece of vintage fabric like the two vintage chiffon hankies shown here that were used as inspiration for these dresses. You may alternatively use chiffon, devoure velvet, an Art Deco print fabric, or anything that evokes the style, print and colour of the twenties.

2. Position pattern on fabric, paying attention to the design of the fabric. Either trace around shape and cut, or carefully pin pattern to fabric and cut out. Do not cut into armhole shaping, cut straight across armhole. You will machine sew around this area before cutting in order to decrease the chance of fraying on straps and shoulders, which will be sewn and joined together after dress is turned and pressed. *Illustration 64.*

3. Machine stitch around entire body of dress leaving small opening near bottom of one side. Turn fabric to right sides carefully, especially if using vintage fabric, as it can be very fragile. Press all seams flat and finish open edge, and pin to hold shape. *Illustration 65.*

4. Topstitch around entire dress to reinforce edges. *Illustration 66.*

5. Fit dress on doll and mark closures at center back opening. Sew shoulder straps together.

Illustration 64

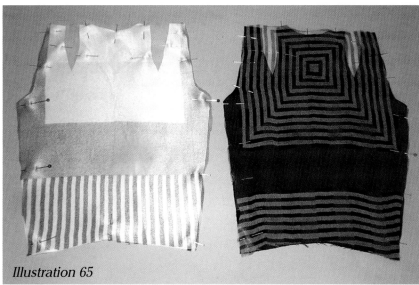

Illustration 65

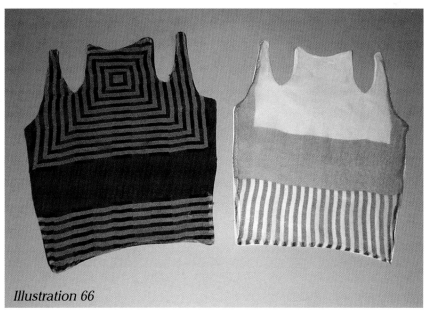

Illustration 66

6. Position the two hanky flounces (cut from corners of the hanky in this case) at lower hip level. Here I've lined it up with the stripe on the chiffon. *Illustration 67.*

7. Add chosen trim and beading at this point. I added peach beads to rosebud centers and strung bead loops to represent leaves radiating from behind the ribbon rose. *Illustration 68.*

8. Bead over flounce. Join at hip to hide stitches and join at shoulder. *Illustration 69.*

9. As a variation to the hanky flounce, an 8in (20cm) length of beaded fringe can be added at hip level. *Illustration 70.*

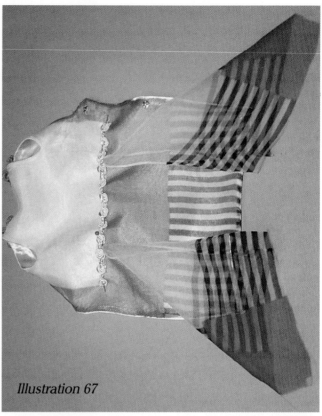

Illustration 67

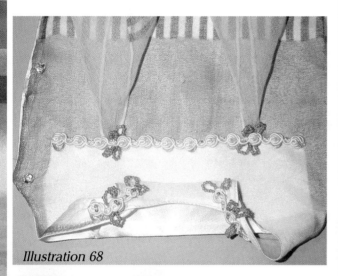

Illustration 68

Illustration 69

Illustration 70

36

Illustration 71

Illustration 72

Headpieces
Illustration 71
The headpieces were made from small pieces of trim, placed around the head, and sewn together where they met at the back. They were then either beaded to match dress or a filigree decoration was added. I glued a small gilt leaf to the center front of metallic ric-rac braid, and then attached a red embroidery stone when glue was dry. The other was just a piece of trim used in the dress beaded to match the beads on the dress. Another variation on a twenties headpiece is made from wire with clusters of beads and filigree vines. *Illustration 72.*

Fans
Illustrations 73, 74 and 75

Fans were made per instructions for fan in Victorian pattern with the exception of the red fan. An old gents tie clip with the fastening removed was used here. The feather was trimmed at the base and glued along length of the pin. Wire was twisted around the base to which some beads were added for the handle.

Illustration 73

Illustration 74

Illustration 75

Illustration 76

Cloche Hat
Illustration 76

Introduced in 1923 by Paris's leading milliner, Caroline Reboux, the cloche style hat became a trademark of the decade. This hat's deep, snug-fitting crown and narrow brim covered the forehead including the eyebrows and concealed the hair to the nape of the neck. Cloches, meaning bell, were made of velvet, satin, rayon faille, straw, horsehair, and felt, and were trimmed in every conceivable manner. They were used for both day and evening-wear.

Note two lengths are given for this cloche hat. One will end at the eyebrows. The longer length will enable you to turn a brim up on the hat. Before cutting fabric, you must decide whether you want a flip brim to center front, to the side, or no brim at all.

1. Cut out main pieces. Using the pattern as guide, sew sides to the back noting length of sides (the front is longer than the back.) Then sew on front section.

2. Sew lining, and with right sides together, sew lining to main piece, sewing around brim edge leaving small opening for turning. Turn hat to right side and turn in raw edges. Finish with tiny slipstitches. Press outer seam flat taking care not to reshape your hat!

Each style suggests various trim ideas. If making a hat with a brim, camouflage the seams by sewing or gluing contrasting appliqués, florals, or geometric motifs making sure glue is dry before trying on your doll's head. You can also embroider small blanket or chain stitches in bright colours all over brim or just in a section. More appliqué or embroidery can be added on the main body of the hat. Egyptian and geometric motifs were fashionable, as was silk ribbon work, flowers and leaves, which were also worked in raffia. Depending on the look you are trying to achieve there are a number of ways to trim your cloche. Look to old 1920's catalogues or vintage magazines to see the decoration on these popular cloches.

Illustration 77. Advertisement showing Cloche hats. Martha Lane Adams Co.

YOU DON'T NEED "READY MONEY" TO GET YOUR FALL HAT!

MAKE THE FIRST PAYMENT AFTER 30 DAYS

Just Write~ "Send It"

No Money Down

Bobbed and Regular HEAD SIZES

Regarding Sizes

For the bobbed hair woman I offer bobbed head sizes (22½ inches)—for the woman who hasn't bobbed hair, there are the regular sizes (23½ inches), and for she who needs an extra large head size (24½ inches) I have hats that will just suit. Refer to page 132 for how to take head measure.

Silk Velvet Poke Bonnet

It takes a new hat to give one the feeling of "all's well with the world." Here's an attractive poke bonnet effect made of good quality silk velvet. It is the short back style that fits so closely to the head and has become ever so popular since bobbed hair has come to stay. The sides and the front of the hat have a brim that is to be reckoned with as far as beauty goes. Across the front of the hat folds of contrasting color silk taffeta appear. Ribozine stitching trims the largest of the folds. At either side there is a large silk velvet poppy. I'll deliver it postage prepaid for your approval.

Colors: Wood brown with crabapple trimming, copen blue with tan trimming or black with copen blue trimming. Regular and bobbed head sizes.

RJ3600. Price, delivered............ **$7.50**

PLEASE NOTE!

Be sure to state correct size and color of the hat you order. If you will do this I guarantee you will be perfectly satisfied.

Mushroom Style— Excellent Quality Silk Velvet

What woman would envy Aladdin his lamp that brought his every wish, when she has CREDIT to fulfill her fondest dreams. You have planned on a new hat for fall, of course. You need one, why not get it? Credit will bring your choice to you at once and you can pay for it as you wear it. Proud will be the woman who chooses this excellent quality silk velvet hat made in the popular mushroom style. The top drapes in soft folds to the side to form a bow effect. An insert of harmonizing color silk taffeta over the crown helps form this bow and draped appearance. A very small brim shades the eyes, though it doesn't exist in the back. Rhinestone pin ornament at front. Credit!

Colors: New blue, black, sand tan or henna. Regular and bobbed head sizes.

RJ3602. Price, delivered... **$6.75**

Bobbed and Regular HEAD SIZES

Bengaline Silk

If you want to be first with the latest style, use your credit and order the hat of your choice. There isn't a woman who wouldn't like this off-the-face bonnet of excellent quality silk bengaline. The crown is the three piece, melon shaped style. Around the entire crown self material folds lend softness and grace and charm. The brim, non-existent in the back, slightly turns up at the front and sides. It is faced with contrasting color silk velvet at the front. Draped about the front of the hat is a chantilly lace veil that just covers the eyes and is certainly a very becoming feature. At either side it is seemingly held in position by clusters of silk flower buds and leaves. At the right side the veil cascades downward in a charming, feminine fashion. Order it now and pay as you wear it.

Colors: Wood brown with crabapple, black with copen blue or new blue with sand trimming. Regular and bobbed head sizes.

RJ3601. Price, delivered........ **$5.45**

Bobbed and Regular HEAD SIZES

Illustration 78. Advertisement showing Cloche hats. Martha Lane Adams Co.

41

Thirties Afternoon Gown
c. 1934

EMBROIDERY IS *THE* NOTE!

CAMILLE

· *Bestway Pattern No. 959.* Post Free Price 1s.

Centre— *Bestway Pattern No. 884.* Post Free Price 1s

VIVIEN

Bestway Pattern No. 960. Post Free Price 1s.

MARGOT

Transfer No. 191. Post Free Price 3d.

Transfer No. 192. Post Free Price 3d.

Transfer No. 193. Post Free Price 3d.

Illustration 79. Embroidery Is the Note illustration showing styles and details of flower embroidery. From Weldon's pattern catalog.

The Thirties could be said to be the era where fashion had the greatest charm and the subtlest innovation. Dresses were ultra-feminine; many gored and cut on the bias, and were in themselves constructional works of art. They flowed and fell around a woman's body, and could be adapted to any physical shape. Gowns for both evening and afternoon were slim, straight and long, with ruffles and frills at the calf or knee, descending to the floor while day dresses were a mere ten inches from the ground. Hats were either miniscule affair's perched over one eye, or large picture hats—a counter-balance for frills and furbelows below.

Illustration 80. Summer dress, 1934. *Costume & Fashion* by James Laver.

Above: Illustration 81. At the races, May 1935. *Costume & Fashion* by James Laver.

Below: Illustration 80. Dresses worn both as day and evening wear. *La Revue de Madame* French magazine.

1930s Bias Cut Dress:

Star Rating **
Modeled by a restyled Breathless Gene® doll
Jewelry by Kim Fisher of The Finishing Touch

Every lady of quality in the thirties knew by now that legs were out and backs were in. Backless, sleeveless, and sporting that new thing called a tan. What better canvas to show off ones diamonds! Strolling to one's box to see one's horse win was such fun, *dahling*!! With such an enormous, lustrous confection of a picture hat, one surely must catch an eye of a Lord or two during Ladies Day at Royal Ascot.

Pattern Pieces:
TR1 Dress
TR2 Bag
TR3 Hat Base

For pattern pieces see page 124

Illustration 83

Materials:
Dress
½ yard/meter chiffon or sheer crepe
½ yard/meter soft poly, or silk satin
cut a 2-½in x 20in (6cm by 51cm) length of chiffon for bottom frill
cut a 1in x 20 in (2.5cm x 51cm) length of chiffon for ruffle
15 tiny ribbon roses, shop bought or make your own
6in (15cm) gold wired ribbon for belt
12in (31cm) fine spaghetti ribbon for straps
2 packs 2mm silk ribbon
variety dusky pink and green micro beads

Hat
1 yard/meter of 3in (8cm) shot metallic organza wired ribbon
1yard/meter of 1-½in (3cm) wired metallic ribbon
1yard/meter of ½in (1.5cm) plain wired ribbon
small pieces of satin for lining base
stiff or heaviest weight of interfacing
2 large pearl-headed pins

Bag
stiff interfacing
satin for lining
10in (26cm) of ½in (1.5cm) organza ribbon
1 ribbon rose
3 flower-shaped beads
selection of micro embroidery beads
1 large glass bead

44

llustration 84

llustration 85

Dress
Illustration 84

1. Cut the two sections of the dress, chiffon and satin, making sure you cut them on the bias of the material following the marking for straight grain on pattern. This will make the dress fluid and stretchy, molding to the doll's curves without the use of darts or tucks. Finish raw edges on chiffon frill and ruffle by machine or hand rolling, or use Fray-check®. Hem satin under-dress and finish hem on chiffon over-dress. Gather top edge of frill 1/2in (1cm) from edge and fit to bottom of chiffon dress using placement line on pattern. *Illustration 85.*

Ilustration 86

2. Gather ruffle and fit to placement line on dress. I added only one ruffle, but more can be added if desired. If you want, additional rows of chain stitch embroidery can be added below ruffle as well. *Illustration 86.*

3. With right sides together, sandwich straps in place by pinning to right sides of satin dress then placing right side of chiffon dress on top. Make sure straps are inside and facing downwards and that they do not get caught in seams while sewing. Sew around neck and front bodice edges. Turn to right side and press. Turn to wrong side again and pin center back seams on satin and chiffon dresses separately. They should only be joined at the bodice seam. *Illustration 87.*

4. Sew center back seams and finish back openings. Add press studs. On front sew ribbon roses in place onto chiffon dress using pattern as a guide. Then loosely twist and catch the 2mm silk ribbon in place with a bead zigzagging up and down the front of the dress and in-between roses. Work 2 rows of ribbon with the second mirroring the first. *Illustration 88.*

Ilustration 87

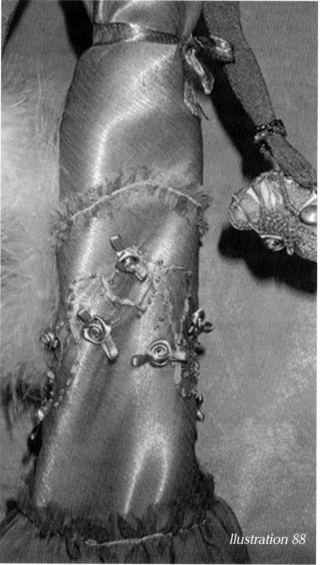

Illustration 88

Picture Hat
Illustration 89

1. Cut circle of interfacing using pattern. Push a long pin through center and secure the ½in (1.5cm) wired ribbon with stab stitches to base. Wrap ribbon around pin without pulling it tight catching with stab stitches at intervals. Twist and shape as you go. Remember you are trying to convey the center of a flower. It does not need to be perfectly in the middle. Slightly off center is pleasing on the eye as are folds and curves. These folds will be pulled out to represent the crown of your hat so leave enough edges free to enable you to do this. Continue to work to outer edge of base and fasten off.

2. Then sew beads into center of flower layering in colours and size as you go. Stamens can be folded in half and stitched to bottom edge at this point. *Illustration 90.*

3. Cut another circle of interfacing slightly larger than the last and using the broadest wired ribbon, start hand-pleating it and laying pinning and sew it around edge of circle. Join raw edges when complete. *Illustration 91.*

Ilustration 89

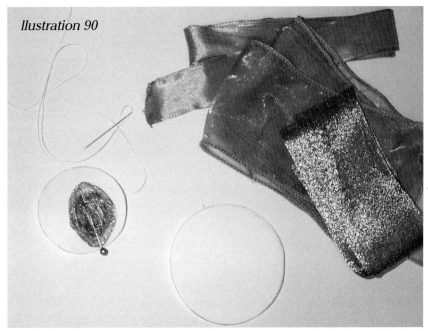

Ilustration 90

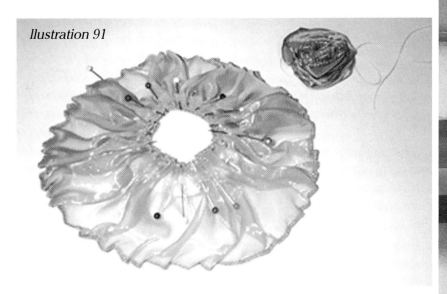

Ilustration 91

llustration 92

llustration 93

4. With narrower contrasting metallic ribbon, hand-pleat and stitch to inside of broad ribbon leaving a space in the middle for flower center. *Illustration 92.*

5. Cover base with fabric turning under raw edges and sewing with tiny slipstitches. *Illustration 93.*

6. Hat can be put onto doll and a variety of positions can be attained because of the wire edges.

7. Be sure to re-pleat or scrunch the edges again after you have played with it.

Bag

1. An old earring I found in a box full of broken jewelry inspired this bag. It was soiled and broken, so I cleaned it up and thought it was just a lovely piece of vintage junk in itself. However, when looking for ideas for the thirties bag, I remembered this little wonder and using the method applied, I recreated it's look into this bag using more or less the same easily obtainable notions. *Illustration 94.*

2. Cut interfacing circle and cover one side with satin. Fold in half with satin to outside of bag. Join edges on each side leaving an open section at top. Work rows of beads and bugles along top edges of bag. Next, take organza ribbon and fold up and down, radiating from central point right across bag. Repeat on other side. Next, sew flower beads to center bottom of bag, then add ribbon rose to middle of base under flower beads. Add more beads if desired. Make long bead handle with large glass bead at center to represent a handle.

llustration 94

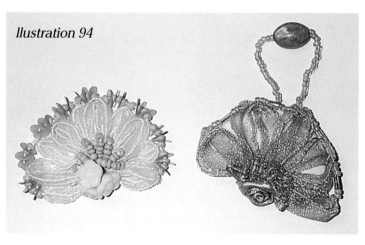

A Southern Belle Dress

Illustration 95

    Hollywood costume epics during the mid to late 1930's led to the promotion of "period chic" influencing women worldwide to dress in historical style like their favorite movie star. Epics such as *Little Women* and *Gone With the Wind* that had outfits designed by Walter Plunkett had their historically correct designs adapted for the retail market. A wide range of fashions and accessories were marketed—dress patterns, hats, veils, snoods, scarves, and jewelry. Printed fabrics, lace ruffles, appliqué, braid and ostrich-feather trimmings, which were inspired by *Gone With the Wind,* were worn well into the 1940's. The Scarlet O'Hara look influenced evening and wedding dresses with cinched in waists and layers of petticoats over crinolines as well as everyday wear such as long hostess or "Day" gowns.

The gray version is a frilled and ruffled confection of silver gray crepe-de-chine with a shimmering silver frilled organza petticoat and organza ruffles around the shoulder line. Her picture hat is made of silver gray cotton and embroidered lace. Her parasol is from crisp white cotton lawn trimmed with cotton Guipure lace. Both are intended to protect her eyes from the blazing Southern sun.

The blue floral printed chiffon version has a simpler white crepe-de-chine bodice that shows off the flattering princess line. It has a matching white petticoat while the large white straw picture hat is trimmed with cotton lace at the crown and gently curves around her face.

The typical 1940's striped hostess gown, reminiscent of Snow White, has a narrower skirt, neater bodice and small puffed sleeves. This dress was made using a piece of vintage striped fabric I found during a rummage through a thrift shop. I thought the colors were so 40's, slightly dull, toned down shades. It shouted "Use me!" so I did. It might not be to everyone's taste, but it captures the essence of the time for me.

Illustration 96

Pattern Pieces:
SC1 Bodice Back & Front
SC2 Side Front
SC3 Flounce
SC4 Sleeve
SC5 Skirt Dimension
SC6 Skirt Dimension (1940's)

For pattern pieces see pages 125-126

Materials:
½ yard/meter of printed chiffon, or
   crepe-de-chine for outer skirt
½ yard/meter of sheer crystal organza,
   cotton, crepe-de-chine for petticoat
¼ yard/meter fabric for bodice (sleeves)
½ yard/meter stripe fabric or typical
   1940's type fabric (for hostess gown
   skirt and sleeves)
1 yard/meter of 3in/8cm cotton lace for
   hat
   selection of laces for trimming
2 yards/meters shoestring ribbon
painted 10in/25cm wooden skewer
large bead
old straw hat (color to compliment or
   contrast with dress fabrics)
strong small elastic band
½ yard/meter satin bias binding to
   match/contrast
straw or dress fabric
fine ribbon or trim to dress hat

Illustration 97

Illustration 98

Dress:

1. Cut relevant pieces for skirt and petticoat and finish raw edges and hems. Finish edges of petticoat frill and gather and fit to petticoat lower edge; stitch in place

2. Join center back seams referring to pattern. Leave back waist open; turn in edges. Slip stitch in place. Note 1940's skirt is shorter and less full than other version. *Illustration 97.*

3. Slip petticoat inside outer skirt and tack together. Treat as one piece for gathering and fitting to bodice.

4. Cut out bodice and bodice lining. Sew in darts on back, stitch the front sides pieces, matching placement dots. If making 1940's dress, sew in darts at either side of bodice front.

5. Join bodice and bodice lining along neck edge, then stitch side seams. Gather skirt and fit to bodice. This is a lengthy job as there is a lot of bulk. A row of machine stitches does help before finally sewing to bodice front.

6. Slip bodice lining over gathered area and slipstitch around waistline seam, catching any raw seams. Sew a length of ribbon around waistline, and sew on press-studs to bodice back. If adding shoulder flounces, finish raw edges, and gather along curved edge. Fit between center front, across shoulder to back opening on each side. *Illustration 98.*

7. Stitch in place and cover stitching with ribbon. Stitch small bow center front and elsewhere if desired i.e. over darts on bodice on 1940's stripe dress.

51

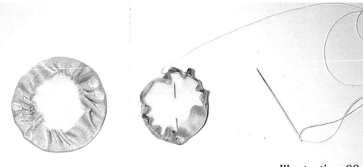

Illustration 99

Hat
Southern Belle Gray Version:

1. Cut two circles, ½in/4cm diameter and 2in/5cm in diameter. Cover both with satin or crepe-de-chine on one side only. *Illustration 99.*

2. Take your gray lace and run a gathering thread along straight edge; pull and form into a circle, joining and finishing edges. *Illustration 100.*

3. Attach the smaller of the two circles into center of lace circle covering gathered section, and sew the larger one to the underside, to act as base of hat. Attach to head by two large pearl-headed pins. *Illustration 101.*

White Straw version
Illustration 102

1. You will need to find an old straw hat for this project that has as fine a weave as possible.

2. Cut off the brim, or outer edge, to leave you with a circle approximately 10in/26cm in diameter. *Illustration 103.*

3. Find a sturdy cylindrical tube about 2in/5cm in diameter. In this case, I used a hard plastic Petit Fours container. Place to center of your hat. *Illustration 104.*

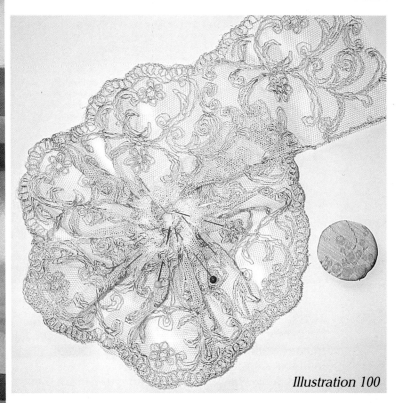

Illustration 100

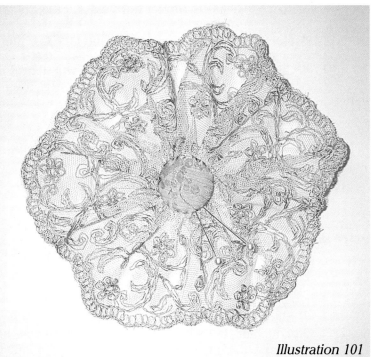

Illustration 101

52

Illustration 102

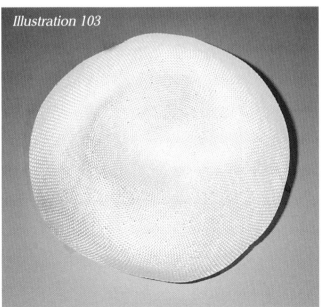

Illustration 103

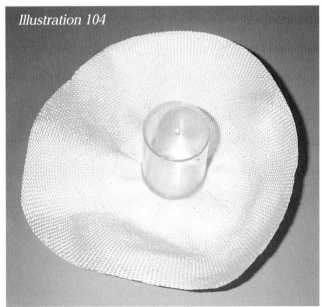

Illustration 104

53

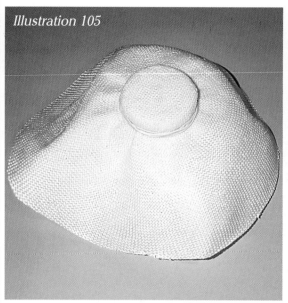

Illustration 105

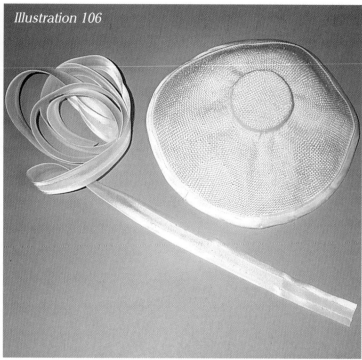

Illustration 106

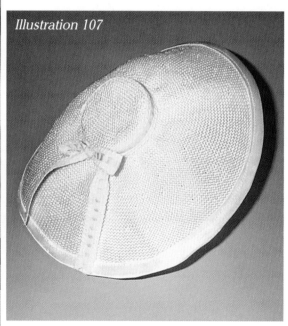

Illustration 107

4. Soak the center of the straw with water until pliable. Pull center over tube, and secure about ¾in/1cm from base with elastic band. I would avoid using any stiffening solution such a starch or a sugar solution because if your doll is wearing her hat in a humid condition, you might just find her hair stuck to the hat. *Illustration 105*.

5. Dry hat thoroughly on mould, drying beside a heater, or with a hair dryer. It must be completely dry before removing elastic band and mold! Resist drying it in the sun, particularly if using a color, as it will fade.

6. Stitch on the satin bias binding around the entire edge of the hat, enclosing top and bottom edges. *Illustration 106*.

7. Attach a ribbon trim around crown sides and tie a bow at back with trailing edges covering join in bias binding. *Illustration 107*.

Parasol
Follow instructions for parasol as given in Edwardian pattern, using coordinating fabrics for your chosen dress.

Simple Snood
1. Cut a circle of net approximately 5in/13cm in diameter, and run a length of ribbon along outer edges.

2. Attach beads to ribbon ends, pull up ribbon and slip it over dolls hair, which you've tied in a ponytail.

3. You can also use milliners netting, or veiling, or use embroidered ribbon, joined in a tube shape, pulled together at base.

4. Then the open edge can be gathered with ribbon, and there you have it, a simple snood. Beads and sequins can be added if the snood is for an evening outfit.

Forties Fashions

The silhouette of the early to mid 40's could best be described as plain and square-shouldered—a utilitarian wartime style. In fact, the two-piece suit more than any other outfit expressed the style of the time. The Second World War dominated the first part of the decade, and women's dresses echoed military uniforms. Fabric was restricted so women used what they had on hand. Therefore, concocted outfits from curtains, tablecloths—anything that could be remodeled and reshaped became a functional fit for any occasion garment. Attention to detail was paramount focusing on seams, pleats, and tucks. Handicrafts flourished like never before as garments were adorned with every conceivable embroidery technique known. Hollywood again played its part brightening up people's lives with its stars swathed in beautiful clothes that were merely a memory to some.

Illustration 108. Suits and cloaks. *Modes au Travaux,* 1939.

Illustration 109. Looking Ahead hats. Fashion Digest, Winter 1941-1942.

Looking Ahead

Designed and made by — Ray Chanda N. Y. School of Modern Millinery

Morning

Afternoon

Evening

Coats

Spectator Sports

Active Sports

Left: Illustration 110. Silhouettes of the Season. Fashion Digest, Winter 1941-1942.

Illustration 111

Illustration 112. Popular bags. Fashion Digest, Winter 1941-1942.

This suit can be made and finished in an endless number of ways. Browse through some old fashion magazines of the forties to get a feel for the detailing, or watch a few early forties movies with stars like Bette Davies or Joan Crawford whose padded shoulders seemed to get wider with every film.

Illustration 113

58

Illustration 114

Pattern Pieces:
FS1 Front/Back Bodice – Back fastening variation
FSb1 Front/Back Bodice – Front fastening variation
FSa1 Front/Back Bodice – Long sleeved variation
FS2 Short Puff Sleeve
FSa2 Long Sleeves
FS3 Skirt
FCL1a Main Body Cloak (without contrasting edging)
FCL2a Yoke Fronts no edging
FCL3a Yoke Back
FCL1b Main Body of Cloak
FCL2b Yoke Fronts &Front Edging
FCL3b Yoke Back
FS4 Oval Crown of hat
FS5 Hat side
FSb2 Bandeaux Hat

Materials:
1-½ yard/meter of main fabric in satin backed
    crepe, velvet, etc.
1-½ yard/meter lining
½ yard/meter contrasting fabric
interfacing
floral appliqué trim
beads, feathers, silk ribbon to trim
small buttons
small piece fine kid leather or faux vinyl skin
small buckle

For pattern pieces see pages 127-132

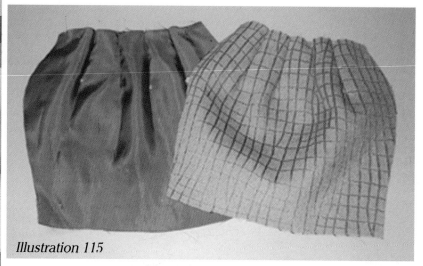

Illustration 115

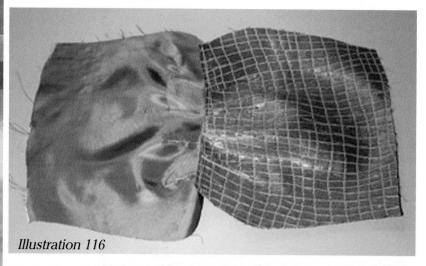

Illustration 116

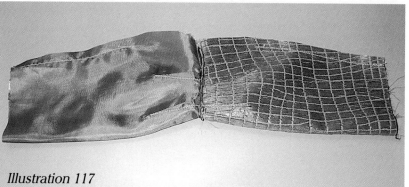

Illustration 117

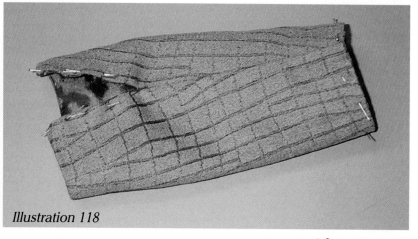

Illustration 118

Skirt:
FS3 Skirt

1. Cut out skirt and lining and sew in darts at waistline. Press set of darts towards the center on lining and other set of darts towards sides on skirt. *Illustration 115.*

2. With right sides together, sew skirt and lining together. Trim seam. Then open and press flat. *Illustration 116.*

3. Join center back seams, trim and press open. *Illustration 117.*

4. Push lining down inside skirt. Turn in raw edges at back opening, turn up hem, and stitch lining to main fabric with slip stitches. Sew on press stud closures at back opening. *Illustration 118.*

Bodice:
FS1 Front/Back Bodice – Back fastening variation
FS2 Short Puff Sleeve
Illustration 119

1. Cut out fronts and back in lining and main fabric, and sew darts. Join back and fronts at shoulder seams and then press. Finish raw edge of lining armhole, as you will not be putting sleeves in the lining. Sew hems at bottom of sleeves and set sleeves into armholes gathering fullness at crown of sleeve. As an alternative, fold fullness in towards center of crown by means of two little tucks. This will produce a more pronounced puff at the shoulder. *Illustration 120.*

2. Finish and press all seams. *Illustration 121.*

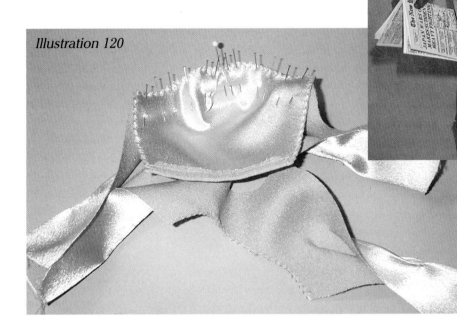

Illustration 119

Illustration 120

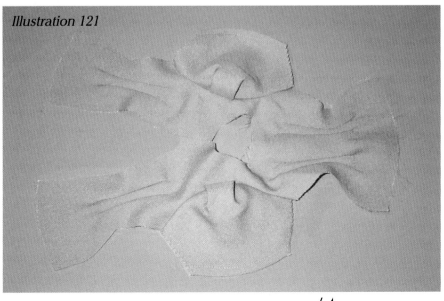

Illustration 121

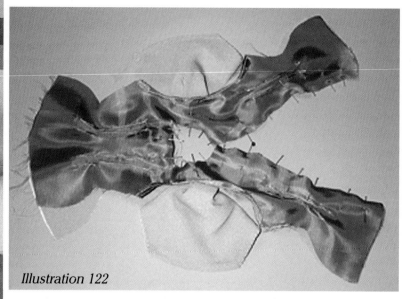

Illustration 122

Illustration 123

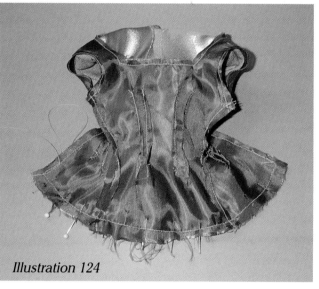

Illustration 124

Illustration 125

3. With right sides together, pin bodice to lining, up center back seams, and around neck edge before you stitch the side seams. This will enable you to have more control when sewing around neck edge. *Illustration 122.*

4. Pin and sew side seams on bodice and lining. *Illustration 123.*

5. Pin lining and bodice along bottom edge and sew. Trim raw edges. Pull work to right side through armholes. Press into shape. *Illustration 124.*

6. To add some embellishment to your jacket, you can either use an embroidered shop bought appliqué trim or you can make your own if you have an embroidery sewing machine. You can also hand-embroider flowers and bead the bodice yourself. If using an appliqué trim, pin it onto bodice while it's on your doll for the best fit. *Illustration 125.*

7. Stitch in place. Add more beads if you wish to enhance or bring out the colours in the embroidery especially around neckline or elsewhere on bodice. Attach silk ribbon bows if desired. *Illustration 126.*

Illustration 126

Illustration 127

FSa1 Front/Back Bodice – Long sleeved variation
FSa2 Long Sleeves
Illustration 127

8. This version has a more tailored fit and long slender sleeves. Make in the same manner as the other two bodices, but note that it doesn't have such a pronounced flare over hip. This version can also be embellished with beads as in this red wool crepe version. *Illustration 128.*

Illustration 128

63

Illustration 129

FSb1 Front/Back Bodice – Front fastening variation
Illustration 129

9. Make as for back fastening bodice, though obviously the press studs are on the front. Choose interesting miniature buttons, diamante, or clusters of beads sewn over press stud stitches. This style also lends itself to a belt, sash or cummerbund. This *Butterscotch* bodice is complimented by a soft gold kid leather belt. *Illustration 130*. Here are two other versions of this suit: *Framboise* a raspberry and black silk suit (*Illustration* 131, note the Black crow on her hat) and *Dans Le Matin* made from a vintage gents silk scarf. The tiny scale and striping add to the detail. *Illustration 132*. The waist is simply cinched in by a satin sash. On her head is a cluster of silk flowers, so reminiscent of 40's millinery.

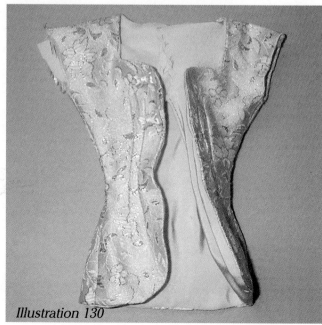

Illustration 130

Illustration 131

Illustration 132

Illustration 133

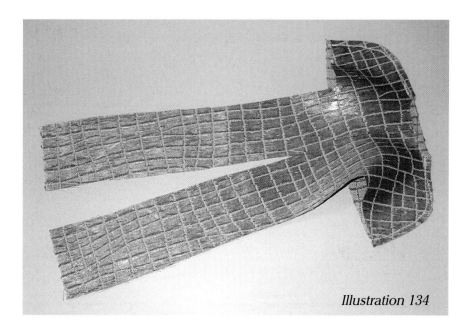

Illustration 134

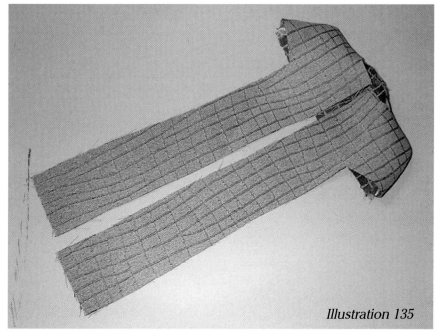

Illustration 135

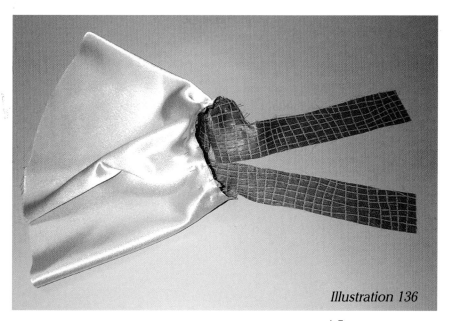

Illustration 136

Cloak:
FCL1a Main Body Cloak
(without contrasting edging)
FCL2a Yoke Fronts no edging
FCL3a Yoke Back

FCL1b Main Body of Cloak
(contrasting edging)
FCL2b Yoke Fronts &
Front Edging
FCL3b Yoke Back
Illustration 133

1. Join fronts and back yoke along shoulder/side seams. *Illustration 134.*
2. Trim raw edges and press, carefully molding shoulder shaping with damp cloth beneath iron. *Illustration 135.*
3. Pin body of cloak to lower edge of cloak matching placement dots on pattern. Make lining to match. *Illustration 136.*

4. Trim and snip into corners to ease stitching and shaping where yoke contrast meets body of cape at center fronts. *Illustration 137.*

5. Trim seams and press flat. *Illustration 138.*

6. Press seams on inside making sure they lie on body of cape and not on the contrasting fabric of yoke. *Illustration 139.*

7. With right sides together, sew cloak to lining leaving a small opening at base center back for turning. Turn to right side and carefully ease out corners. Press all seams flat. Sew hook and bar closures at neckline. *Illustration 140.*

Illustration 137

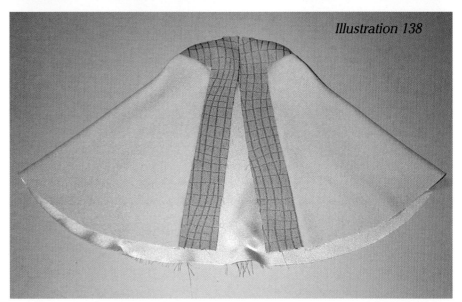

Illustration 138

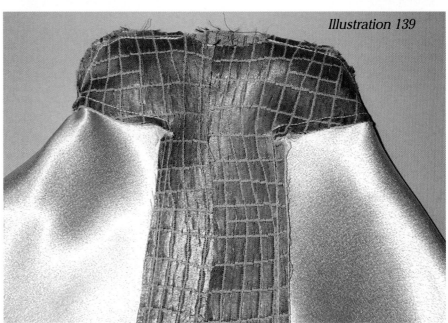

Illustration 139

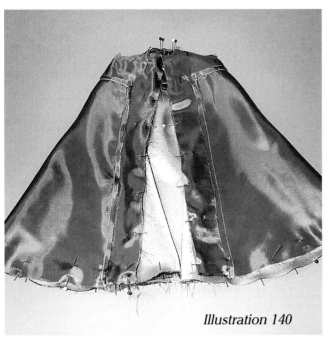

Illustration 140

I've also included a pattern for a cloak that has no contrast center front panels. This is a lot easier to construct since you have no complex corners to sew around. Madra® is seen here wearing a claret velvet cape made from this pattern to which I've added some embroidery. Note too, her hat, which is a smaller version of the thirties hat made with claret wired ribbon and beaded with wine and green beads. Her skirt has been lengthened using the same straight skirt pattern by just adding a few extra centimeters. The bodice is the 50's Baby Dress bodice finished off at lower waist edge. So by mixing patterns you can dramatically achieve new looks. *Illustration 141.*

Illustration 141

Illustration 142

Bandeaux Hat:
FSb2 Bandeaux Hat

This type of bandeau hat is reminiscent of medieval head dresses. In fact, there were other fashion styles from this period revived and made popular again—snoods and monks cowl drapes to name but two. This bandeaux is easily made by sewing a piece of plastic coated wire across middle of bandeaux shape interfacing, which is then covered with fabric, to back and front. Add sequins, stones or beads sewn on in a pattern of your choice. The bandeaux can then be bent or molded into your desired position depending on your doll's hair. A gold snood can also be attached to either end, and the hair slipped inside as in this outfit. The snood is made from a circle of gold netting. *Illustration 142*. Another example of this type of beaded bandeaux can be seen with my *Chrysanthe* outfit beaded to look like Chrysanthemums. *Illustration 143*.

Illustration 143

70

Illustration 144

Oval Hat:
FS4 Oval Crown of hat
FS5 Hat side
Illustration 144

To make this small cap that sits at the front of your doll's head, cut main fabric, lining, and interfacing. Sew main fabric to side piece and crown interfacing. Then line. Join side piece by folding lengthwise and sewing together with slipstitches. Then form into an oval shape and attach crown to this again using tiny slipstitches. Add ribbon trim, beads or feathers to coordinate with your outfit. *Illustration 145.*

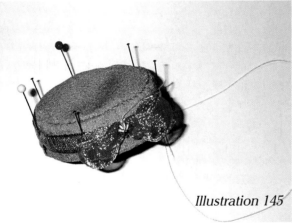

Illustration 145

Clutch Purse
Choose a purse pattern and cut interfacing, lining, and main fabrics according to pattern. Sew main fabric to interfacing, line, and then fold in half. Join side seams and bead as you wish adding a beaded handle or straps as desired. *Illustration 146.*

Illustration 146

71

Wrap
Illustration 147

Cut rectangle of fabric approximately 20in (51cm.) Fold in half lengthwise and stitch together leaving opening to turn. Turn to right side, press, and add beads to bottom edges, which will add weight to your wrap. It will then fall better from your doll's shoulders without having to pin it on.

Illustration 147

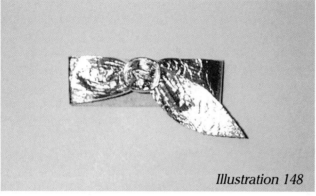
Illustration 148

Belt
Illustration 148

Using pattern, cut belt shape from kid leather, faux leather, or vinyl from an old purse. Fold one end around the center of tiny buckle and glue in place.

Gauntlet Gloves

Cut a piece of Lycra or nylon fabric. Hem along one edge. Then draw around card glove template. Slowly stitch around shape; then trim close to stitching and turn right side out. Bead along one edge if you wish, or stud with beads. All other gloves shown in this book are made in this way. Just lengthened or shortened to suit outfit. *Illustration 149.*

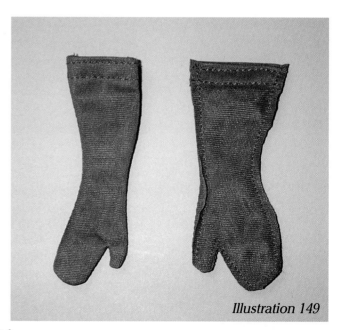
Illustration 149

Star Rating **

This outfit consists of a tight fitting, two-tone, sheath dress underneath a deceptively easy short faux-fur cape, which in the 40's might have been monkey fur or fox. The beading around the hip-line covers the seam line, which joins the two fabrics and could so easily be interpreted in so many ways. Your colour combinations could change just as easily—black/white; black/red; navy/pink; chocolate brown/olive; gray/lilac—to name but a few.

Pattern Pieces:
FTTD1 Skirt Front
FTTD2 Skirt Back
FTTD3 Bodice Back
FCA1 Cape Side
FCA2 Cape Back

Materials:
¼ yard/meter black wool crepe
¼ yard/meter camel wool crepe
¼ yard/meter lining
¼ yard/meter faux fur fabric
12in (31cm) ready sewn bugle bead trim
interfacing
black beads sequins

Illustration 150

73

Illustration 151

Dress:
FTTD1 Skirt Front
FTTD2 Skirt Back
FTTD3 Bodice Back
llustration 151

1. Sew black and camel, front and sides together. Sew in darts. Sew darts in lining.

2. Join shoulder seams on both dress and lining. Sew center back seams. *Illustration 152.*

3. Place both bodice and lining right sides together, pin, and sew around neckline. Trim and cut into the curves. Sew small, tacked hem along armhole edges of lining and bodice. *Illustration 153.*

4. Sew side seams on both dress and lining. Turn right side out and press. Finish center back seam opening slipstitching bodice to lining. Then slipstitch bodice to lining at armholes, removing tacking thread. Try on doll and mark for closures. *Illustration 154.*

5. Take the bugle bead trim and sew across bodice/skirt seam from center back to center back. Or you can sew you own beads or braid over seam line. *Illustration 155.*

6. Take a selection of black sequins, beads and bugles and sew above bugle trim on bodice. *Illustration 156.*

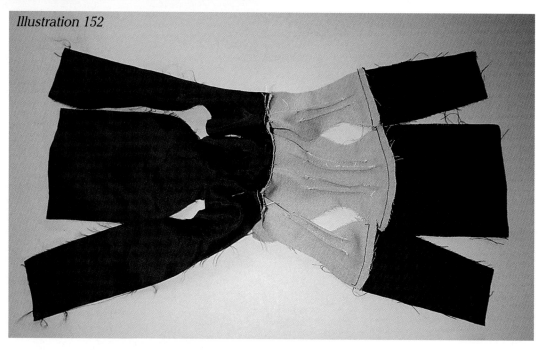

Illustration 152

Illustration 153

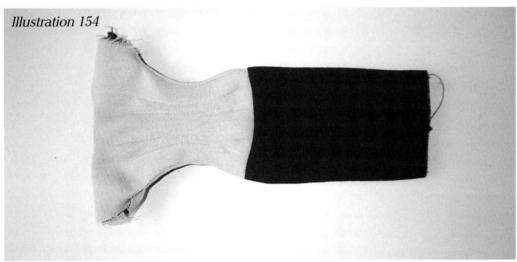

Illustration 154

Illustration 155

Illustration 156

Illustration 157

Illustration 158

40's Bird Hats
Illustrations 157 and 158

The Forties was a decade renowned for it's very silly hats. They provided some lighthearted relief from the stresses of life considering the world around the wearer was at war. Hats were made from everything you could imagine. Anything could be plunked on top of a woman's head in the name of fashion. I used small mushroom birds on some of my hats as they are ridiculously cheap, bright, colourful, the right scale, and very easy to sew or glue in place. They can be bought at craft supply stores, usually in packets of two or more, in every conceivable colour and shape. You simply need a piece of braid formed into a circle to which you sew some veiling and some silk flowers for the bird to perch in. Then you sew or glue on your bird. *Illustration 159*. A very easy hat and a true 40's fashion statement!

Illustration 159

Illustration 160

Plumed Hat
Illustration 160

1. Gather all your materials to make this hat: black long silk petals, small silk flowers, black and pewter beads and bugles, black netting, cord hat base with veiling attached (directions for this type of base are in the "Fun in the Fifties" section.)
2. Gradually layer trims from the back with large petals first, then smaller flowers attaching loops of beads from centers, then rows of gray beads radiating from flowers to front of hat.

Hair Decoration

This was a period when a lady always wore something in her hair or on her head when going out. Often, real flowers were formed into corsages that were pinned into coiled plaited hair or rolled hairstyles that were so popular then. The headpiece shown here is described in detail in the Victorian section. I used vintage blue velvet flowers and gold beads and leaves. I also dipped each leaf in poly-flakes, the ultra fine glitter used by egg crafters for added sheen and sparkle. This headpiece is worn with a gold brocade cloak and dress that are trimmed and lined with ice blue crepe-de-chine. This outfit is named *That Midas Touch* and was made for the Gene® Convention competition, Chicago 2000. *Illustration 161.*

Illustration 161

Illustration 162

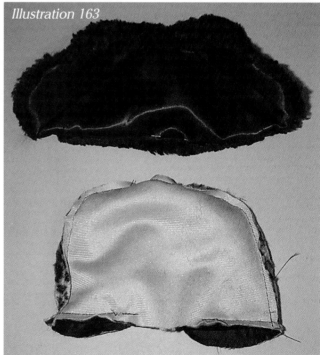

Illustration 163

Cape
FCA1 Cape Side
FCA2 Cape Back
Illustration 162

1. Cut out front sides and back from faux fur and lining. Take care when cutting fur that you cut it with the pile (the way the fur lies,) and you cut with the fur laying downwards towards bottom or hemline of cape. Use sharp embroidery scissors to actually cut out your fur shapes, clipping rather than cutting through fabric, as this will prevent your fur pile on right side from having a rather blunt cut. Join shoulder/side seams on cape and lining. *Illustration 163.*

2. Sew lining to main fur part. Then when turned to right side, press very lightly into shape under a dry cloth, so as not to flatten pile completely or singe pile if synthetic fibers.

Fun in the Fifties

Illustration 164. Popular 1950s accessories. *Woman's Illustrated.*

The stiff masculine cut of the Forties was replaced with womanly curves, hugely full-swinging skirts, darted and shaped bodices, and an emphasis on the waist, with women lacing themselves again into corsets, "waspies", to achieve the "New Look." Christian Dior, the "King" of Parisienne couture, reigned over a decade of intense excitement and fashion activity creating a new line almost every season. The "Princess" line, in 1951, was beautifully cut with long seams running down a waistless dress that flared out gracefully to end at mid-shin level. The soft-shouldered look of the H-line of 1954, and the Y and the A-line in 1955 consisted of a dress or a jacket and skirt in a pronounced flaring line with a horizontal stroke of flat pleats breaking out where the stroke of a capital letter H would be. Balenciaga, Balmain, Hubert de Givenchy, Charles James, Jacques Fath are all names we associate with the 1950's. Their names conjure up images of either huge sculptured ball gowns or simply little black suits.

Illustration 165. Debbie Reynolds wearing Baby dresses. *Picture Show* magazine.

This is a very simple dress to make and the possibilities it offers to adapt and change the look are endless. Look to movies of the 50's to inspire you. Look at old magazines, especially pattern magazines of the time, which are simply full of these "Baby" dresses. I looked for a plausible explanation as to why they were called this, but can only imagine they are similar in style to those dresses in which you would dress a child, or maybe it was because it was a shorter version of the full length ball gown so popular in the 50's. I have a feeling the latter may be the most reasonable answer. These dresses were made in every conceivable fabric to suit all seasons and situations. Indeed, you could add a straight skirt to this bodice. Then add the full skirt with the opening center front for a completely different look. The choice is yours—just experiment!

Illustration 166

Pattern Pieces:
BD1 Skirt
BD2 Bodice
BD4 Petticoat (optional)

For pattern pieces
see pages 133-137

Materials:
1-½ yard/meter of silk, satin, crepe-de-chine, printed chiffon or
  similar for main skirt
1-½ yard/meter of satin for bodice and lining of skirt
beads, pearls, sequins to trim
1/3 yard/meter finest weight upholstery cording
feathers, veiling, embellishments to trim

Baby Dress Circular Skirt:
Illustration 166

1. Cut two pieces of circular skirt—the lining and your main fabric. Sew center back seams to point indicated on pattern. Press seams flat. With right sides together, and on a flat surface, pin each piece together around hemline. *Illustration 167.*

2. Sew around edge, then trim fabric and turn skirt to right side. Press edge carefully. Finish lining and main fabric at center back opening. Then tack around waistline edge. *Illustration 168.*

3. Cut two bodice pieces, sew darts, and press flat. *Illustration 169.*

4. Trim excess fabric from dart to reduce bulk at waistline and to prevent bulge showing through when pressed.

5. Sew bodice lining and main fabric together, turn to right side and press.

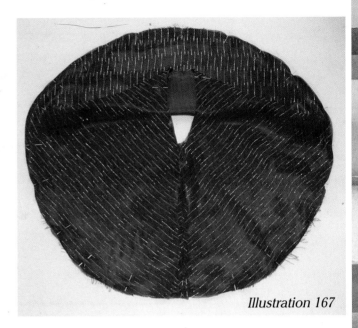

Illustration 167

Illustration 168

Illustration 169

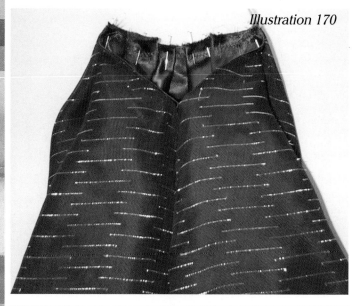
Illustration 170

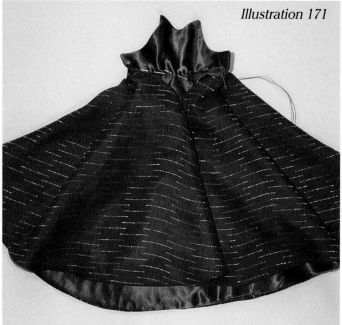
Illustration 171

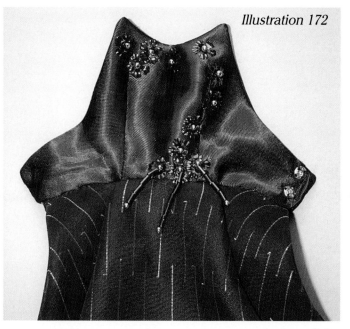
Illustration 172

Illustration 173

6. Pin center front of bodice to skirt center front, then gradually decrease fullness of skirt by folding and hand-tucking pleats around waist until the skirt waist fits the bodice. Carefully stitch skirt to bodice front leaving lining unattached. *Illustration 170.*

7. Press waistline seam and trim excess fabric. Stitch bodice lining to waistline stitching line concealing raw edges beneath with tiny slipstitches. *Illustration 171.*

8. Petticoat can be added if wished following instructions 6 & 7 given for straight skirt or can be omitted for a more slender look

9. Sew press studs to bodice. Bead front of bodice as desired. Here, I've sewn flower sequins liberally across front secured by tiny navy beads adding beads and straps. The possibilities are endless. *Illustration 172.*

10. Evening wraps can be made quite easily by cutting 2 rectangular lengths of cloth 20in (50cm) long, sewing together, turning, and pressing flat. Then you can leave as is or gather each end and add a beaded tassel. *Illustration 173.*

You can alter the bodice quite easily by cutting straight across instead of cutting downwards at center front. You can then cut a contrasting lining, which when sewn, can be turned downwards at bust line and beaded or left plain if a print is used. The tips of each bodice point can be turned down and beaded or ribbon or bead straps attached. The following examples show the Baby Dress pattern used with a variety of different fabrics and trims:

Illustration 174. Baby dress of lemon organza with tiny white flock dots, satin bodice with daisies scattered across ribbon, which attaches to bodice like a halter neck.

Illustration 175. Baby dress in dramatic gold and black print chiffon with black and gold accessories.

1950's Accessories:
Illustration 176
Selection of navy accessories to go with navy Baby dress, hat, gloves, jewelry, navy satin clutch purse.

Illustration 176

1950's Cord Hat with Variations

1. Cut a length of cord 12in (30cm) long, and sellotape each end to stop fraying. Gradually start to wind cord into a spiral, stitching each side together as you go so it does not unwind. Catch ends to one side and bind off. You should now have a little cartwheel cap/hat shape to work with. *Illustration 177.*

2. If you want a veil on your hat, cut a small rectangle of tulle or millinery net and sew it to one side of your hat, gathering edges as you go and stitching to underside of your hat. *Illustration 178.*

3. To line your hat, cut a little circle of satin slightly larger than your hat and sew to underside of hat securing in the raw edges and gathered pieces of net with small stitches.

4. Once your lining and veiling is securely sewn on, you can then go on to decorate your hat base any way you choose. The white base has peach silk flowers and petals clustered towards the back secured by pearls, whereas the navy base has a feather secured by flower sequin shapes. *Illustration 179.*

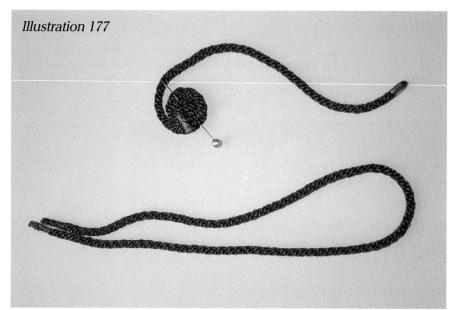

Illustration 177

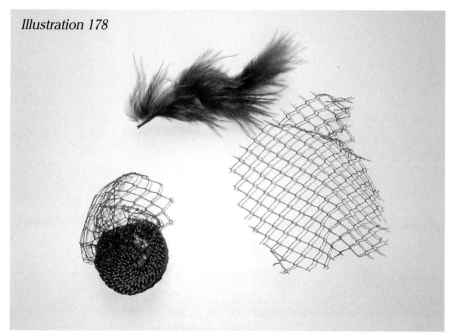

Illustration 178

Illustration 179

The following hats all started life with a hat base made with these instructions, but each hat, with the aid of different embellishments, can look entirely unique. Look for cord that already has other colours combined, i.e. gold thread, which will add interest and decrease the amount of beading you need to do.

Illustration 180. Black base covered at front with gold bugles with a piece of black gold-edged chiffon pleated and secured to rear with more bugles.

Illustration 181. Wine and gold cord base with piece of black marabou trim secured to back with large wine pearl beads clustered around.

Illustration 182. Royal cord base covered in a variety of blue and jade beads with a bright jade feather to rear.

Illustration 183. Black base with padded red silk oval, red black net veiling and beaded to look like a ladybug!

Tight fitting beaded sweaters and cardigans were very popular in the 1950's, as women tried to identify with such screen goddesses as Jayne Mansfield or Jane Russell who wore skin tight clothes and stiletto-heeled shoes. In this design, I've just beaded a short bolero jacket, but you could easily use the same method for a tighter longer cardigan that would button up the back, a style that was itself popular then.

Pattern Pieces:
Bolero:
KB1 Back
KB2 Sides
KB3 Sleeves
Baby Dress:
BD2 Bodice
BD3 Skirt
BD4 Petticoat

Materials:
fine knit garment
¼ yard/meter satin for bodice and jacket lining
¼ yard/meter polyester silk, crepe-de-chine
¼ yard/meter net or tulle
selection fine trims, braids
beads pearls sequins to trim jacket
net or milliners veiling
silk flower, feathers etc. to trim hat
plastic coated wire (you can find this holding toys inside their packaging)

Illustration 184

Beaded Bolero
Illustration 184
(see illustrations below for ideas of beading for knit jacket)

This is the cheater's way to make a knit bolero jacket without knitting it by hand or struggling with minute pins and needles and tiny stitches. But that doesn't mean you have to own up to this fact!

1. Select a knitted garment made from very fine yarn, cotton or acrylic with very fine stitches. Ideally it will have a finished edge rather than starting with a ribbed edge. Once you have found this, hand launder in lukewarm water, dry flat, and gently press. Using pattern made into card templates, trace outlines onto knitted fabric making sure you place the back and sleeve bottom edges against a finished edge.

Ideas for beading knit jacket

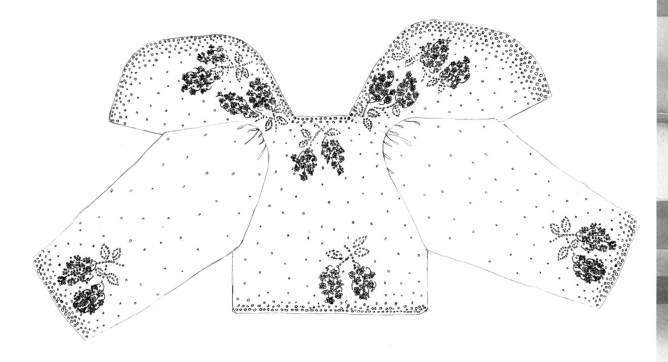

2. Carefully serge or run a zig-zag stitch around the traced lines before you cut anything out. Then very carefully cut around the stitches. Stitch shoulder seams together. Cut out satin lining, join shoulder seams, and finish shoulder seam edge, as there are no satin sleeves in lining. *Illustration 185.*

3. Fit in sleeves, and press.

4. Stitch side seams on both knit jacket and lining. Then fit lining to knit jacket turning in and pinning raw edges around front and back as you go. Stitch in place with tiny slipstitches. *Illustration 186.*

5. Try your jacket on the doll. If, at this point, you decide you don't want a curved edge, you can fold over a revere so that it looks like a satin lapel, which you should stitch in place. Press lining and outer seams gently. *Illustration 187.*

6. Select beads, pearls or other embellishments for your jacket. Sew your beads onto the body of the jacket carefully avoiding catching lining on inside, or sewing sleeves together inside! You can sew them on randomly or follow some of the ideas given in the previous illustrations.

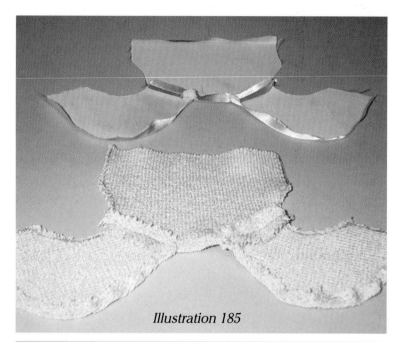

Illustration 185

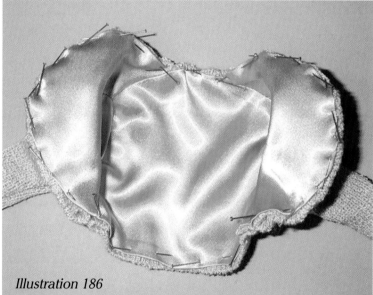

Illustration 186

Illustration 187

Illustration 188

Baby Dress Straight Skirt

1. Cut skirt using dimensions given on pattern BD3. I've used a printed blouse I found in a thrift shop, which had an intriguing miniature print and a row of tucks running vertically down the center front. So I used these tucks in the bottom of my skirt carefully measuring and cutting my rectangle to required size and remembering to include hem allowance.

2. Make bodice following the instruction for Baby dress with circular skirt bodice instructions steps 3 – 5.

3. This skirt does not have a lining as such, but the method of attaching this skirt to the bodice is the same as for the circular skirt, so follow those instructions, steps 6 and 7.

4. Once the bodice is attached, the lining is stitched in place, and the studs are attached, add a daisy trim to the waist along bust line and back. *Illustration 188.*

5. Leave two lengths, which will be joined to back bodice forming the straps. *Illustration 189.*

6. Cut out petticoat from fine net or tulle and trim with lace using placement lines on pattern.

7. Fit petticoat to inside of skirt, and pin to waistline easing in any fullness with a little hand tuck. Then slipstitch in place. *Illustration 190.*

Illustration 189

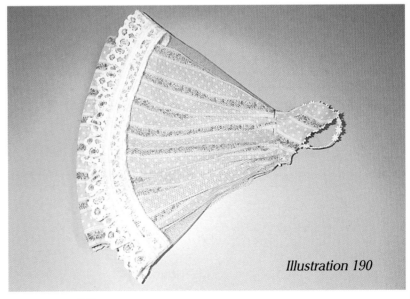

Illustration 190

Hat

1. Cut two 2-½in (6cm) pieces of ½in (1cm) velvet ribbon. Cut two pieces of stiff interfacing the same length as the ribbon, and stitch a piece of plastic coated wire down the center. Trim the interfacing a little so it is slightly narrower than the ribbon. *Illustration 191.*

2. Sew the velvet ribbon to interfacing with the wire lying in between the two. Then sew two pieces of satin ribbon onto interfacing sides, turning in raw edges at both ends. *Illustration 192.*

3. Select a few silk flowers and leaves that compliment the colors in the dress or jacket fabric. Cut two lengths of crepe-coated wire, and sew to center of velvet ribbon. This will be your flower stems.

4. Sew leaves and flowers onto the ends of each piece of velvet ribbon covering green stem. Sew beads into the centers of these silk flowers. *Illustration 193.*

5. Join the two velvet bars in the center to form an X shape. Cut a circle of net or tulle approx. 3in (8cm) in diameter. Gather across the center and stitch to underside of X shape.

6. Pull net up between velvet bars, and use large pearl-headed pins to secure the hat to your doll's head. *Illustration 194.*

7. Try the hat on your doll's head, and mould it to fit snugly to the front or rear depending on your doll's hairstyle, pulling and shaping the veiling to suit.

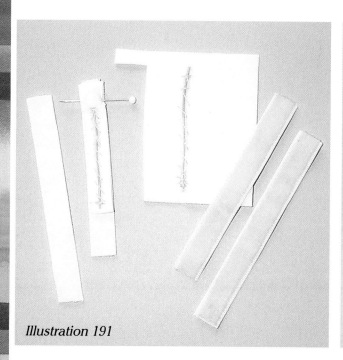

Illustration 191

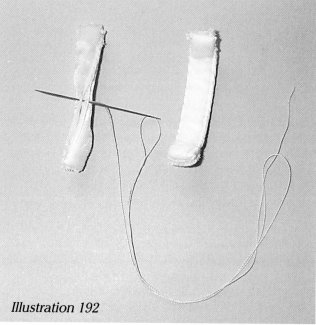

Illustration 192

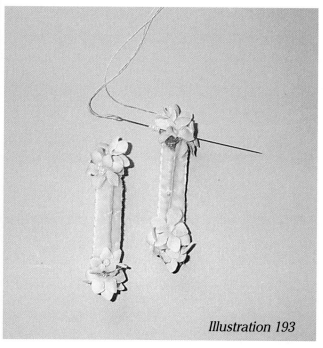

Illustration 193

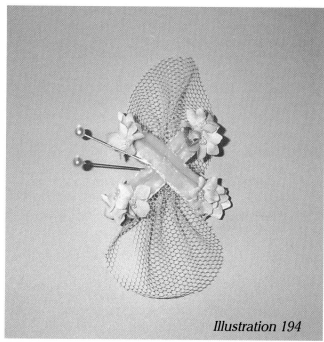

Illustration 194

Bag

1. Find two square or rectangular flat earrings that match your dress and jacket fabric colours. Remove the clips or stud backing with pliers, and file smooth.
2. Trace around these shapes onto stiff card, and cut out shapes using a craft knife. Then glue to each earring back. Take a length of fine gilt chain and glue each end to top corner of one piece of card. *Illustration 195.*

3. Glue the two earrings together taking care not to catch the chain in between, as this will be your bag strap. Use a heavy-duty clip to secure pieces together until they are completely dry. *Illustration 196.*
4. These earrings had a silver metal finish, but my chain was gilt, so I painted the metal with gold acrylic to match. You can then finish with an acrylic gloss or matte varnish to seal paint. *Illustration 197.*

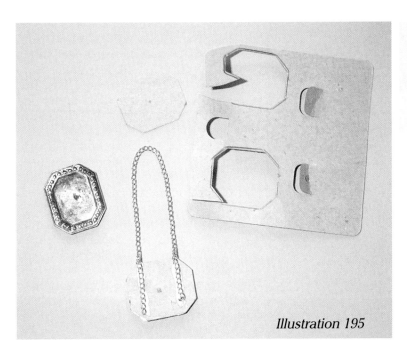

Illustration 195

Illustration 196

Illustration 197

Illustration 198

Short, very short boleros, were popular as was the art of "bust draping". Chiffon was pleated across the bust, tulle was draped and gathered across the bust, in fact, fabric was draped over, under and around the bust in every conceivable way. This jacket closes tightly, right under the bust line, emphasizing the bodice of the dress beneath. I've emphasized the bust even more so by adding a tulle "bra", which hides your doll's modesty if she's at all nervous about all this attention to her cleavage. The dress is also fitted to the hipline this time, hugging her contours, before flaring out to a gathered skirt. The skirt's decoration can be handled in a variety of ways. Indeed, if you can find an embroidered fabric that you can further embellish, then this is another option. Just have fun creating.

Pattern Pieces:
FJ1 Crop Jacket
FJ2 Dress Bodice Front
FJ3 Dress Bodice Back
FJ4 Skirt Dimensions

Materials:
1/4 yd/meter of velvet for jacket
1/4 yd/meter lining for jacket
1/2 yd/meter of silk dupion, satin
   or crepe-de-chine for dress
net or tulle for petticoat, hat and
   "bra" insert
silk flowers, ribbon, beads for hat
embroidery cotton, or silk ribbon
fabric paints or pens
heavy weight interfacing
1/2 yd/meter of 1/2 in (1cm) velvet
   and satin ribbon

For pattern pieces
see pages 136-137

Strapless Dress

1. Cut out the four bodice sections and sew in darts. Then join side seams and press flat. Now join front to lining starting at center back seam, around bodice and down other back seam. Turn right side out and press.

2. Mark out area for skirt on fabric. Now you can either embroider flowers onto skirt or you can hand-paint stems with fabric paint or pens. Then appliqué organza flowers as in cream silk version, or you can embroider silk ribbon flowers, leaves and stems. *Illustration 198.*

3. Join center back seam. Pin bodice onto doll marking back closures, sew on press studs.

4. Take bodice off the doll, and with studs still fastened, pin skirt to bodice pinning center front and back seams first. Gradually pin skirt onto bodice taking in fullness by working little pleats and pinning as you go. Stitch skirt to bodice front. Then slipstitch lining in place securing raw edges between fabrics.

5. A tulle petticoat can then be stitched in place. Cut a similar piece of net using skirt pattern, but slightly shorter. Gather to fit and then slipstitch in place. This is purely optional as you might not want such a full skirt depending on what type of fabric you chose as your dress fabric. *Illustration 199.*

6. On back of dress, a double row of pearls can be added to look like pearl buttons, while on the front, the top of the bodice can be folded and beaded as on cream silk dress.

7. If you dislike your doll showing this much cleavage, you can add a rectangle of net 3-½in x 2in (9cm x 5cm) that you've gathered together at center front and at both ends. Place this on inside of the dress at bust line. It is easier to do this on the doll. *Illustration 200.* Once you're sure you have a nice snug fit over the bust, sew the net "bra" to bodice at sides and center front. Choose a coordinating colour for the net and make it a feature.

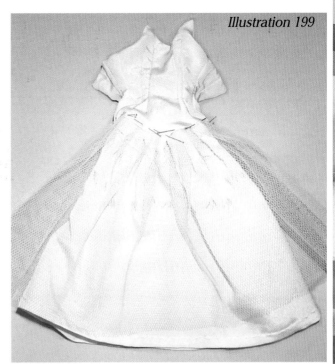

Illustration 199

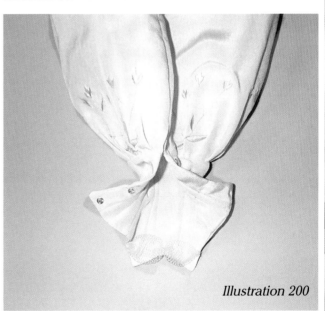

Illustration 200

Illustration 201

Floral Veil
Illustration 201

Many so-called hats in the 1950's were nothing more than pieces of milliners net decorated with bows, flowers, feathers or fur. These tiny pieces of frippery were pinned to the hair, and worn with all sorts of attire, both indoor and out. Here, I've just cut an oval of net, roughly 5in (13cm). First, I folded it in half. Then I gathered across the straight edge, pulled it tight, and then decorated the center with a clump of silk flowers. Beads, pearls and bows were then stitched in place for added interest.

Crop Jacket
Illustration 202

1. Cut two pieces of fabric, brocade and lining, and stitch in the darts on shoulder, and bust.

2. Turn back hems on sleeves and stitch. Then finish/serge raw edges and press flat. Stitch underarm seams.

3. With wrong sides together, attach lining to brocade pinning and machine stitching around entire front, sides and back. Pay special attention to shaping of narrow front fastening.

4. Turn work right side out pulling through armholes. Then carefully prize front under-bust fastening into shape using a long blunt instrument (a chopstick works well.)

5. Try jacket on doll. Pin sleeves to lining adjusting under-arm seams so they match. Then mark where press studs have to go on the under-bust fastening. Take off doll, slipstitch sleeve hems, and add press studs to front closure. *See Illustration 203.*

Illustration 202

Illustration 203

Embroidery for 1950s Strapless Dress
Hand-paint then stitch on applique flower or embroider by satin stitch or use silk ribbon embroidery.

repeat design

on fold

Illustration 204. Front view of embroidered strapless dress. *Jewelery by Bijoux Fantasié.*

Illustration 205. Back view of embroidered strapless dress.

The Swinging Sixties

Designers working for the ready-to-wear market dominated the Sixties. Fashion was focused predominantly on teenagers and styles for everyone, not just the rich and famous. London seemed to be the center of the fast turn-around styles, with Mary Quant, Ossie Clark, and Zandra Rhodes ahead of the pack. Chelsea was in, as was Carnaby Street and King's Road. Street fashion was born, literally. A stiff, geometric, or see-through mini, midi or maxi was "right on." Tights were in, stockings out. Pinafores, balaclavas, paper, metal, patent leather, embroidered sheepskin—anything and everything was used. Pop artists created ultra-psychedelic art that was conveyed into fabric colours and prints. Glitz, sequins, and metallic fabrics heralded the Glam Rock of the 1970's. As they said, "Rock on."

Simple Sixties Halter Dress c. 1966
Going to A - Go - Go

Star Rating *
Modeled by Daisy and Willow

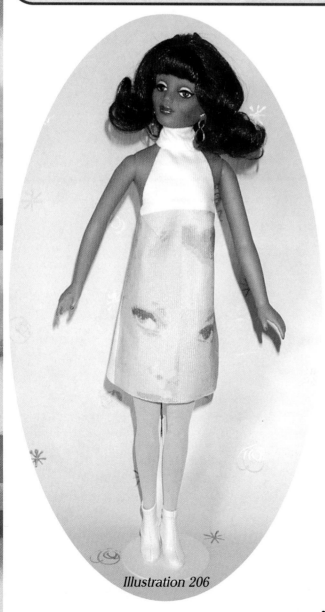

Illustration 206

Take two girls and put them in simple shift dresses. One has a psycho-pop art print, just like a wearable Andy Warhol, and the other wears a fringed sequined affair. Now they're both ready to hit Club-land and shimmy and shake with the best of them—maybe to a little Beatles or The Dave Clark Five.

Pattern Pieces:
DW1 A-Line Dress
DW1a Straight Dress
DW2 Halter Collar
DW3 Stocking

For pattern pieces see page 138

Materials:
¼ yard (30cm) of white cotton lawn, or black satin (or colour of your choice)
2 yard/meters of fringed sequin trim
unused stockings or tights

Poster Print A-Line Dress:
Illustration 206

1. Take a colour picture of a face approximately 4in x 5in (10cm x 13cm) and using a Photo effect program, alter it to look like a 60's Pop Art painting. A good print shop should be able to do this for you. Now get a few colour photocopies of it. *Illustration 207.*

2. Ask the print shop to transfer your image onto computer transfer paper, reminding them to reverse the image, as anything you iron onto fabric will be reversed. This is essential if letters or words are involved. Cut out your photo, leaving a little border for pulling off backing paper, but follow the instructions given by the manufacturer.

3. Care must be taken when ironing print onto paper. If iron is not held on long enough or there is uneven pressure, the transfer print will not adhere evenly to your fabric like the blue example on the left. However, if the iron is left on for too long, the paper will stick to the fabric as in the pink example on the right. *Illustration 208.*

4. This shows a finished print with sample print to the side for comparison. *Illustration 209.*

5. Using A-Line pattern template, place it over printed fabric in desired position. In this instance, the top of the print is lined up with the bust line and armhole shaping.

If you are making the black satin spangled sequin dress, continue with steps 6 – 10. *Illustration 210.*

Illustration 207

Illustration 209

Illustration 210

Illustration 208

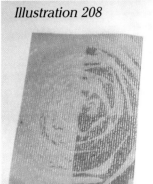

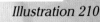

97

Sequin Spangled Halter Dress:
Illustration 211

6. Using pattern DW1a cutting lines to create a straighter dress, cut out dress in black satin. Sew in darts, then pin around entire edge from neck opening to neck opening on opposite side. Turn to right side through neck opening and press flat. *Illustration 212.*

7. Fold halter collar in half with right sides together. Stitch each side between dots. Turn to right side and press. *Illustration 213.*

8. Slip open edge over neck opening with right side of dress facing and stitch in place. Press seam and fold under raw edge on collar. Slipstitch open edge to wrong side of dress at throat. Sew hook and eye closure at back neck edge and press studs at center back edges. *Illustration 214.*

Illustration 212

Illustration 211

Illustration 213

Illustration 214

9. Using a sequined trim, pin rows in place starting at base of skirt and work upwards. Or alternatively, bead the dress yourself covering it with tiny flowers or sew on your own fringing and bead trims. *Illustration 215.*

10. Optional - Stitch a strip of sequin trim around base of halter, or leave plain, or add your own beaded trim. *Illustration 216.*

Illustration 215

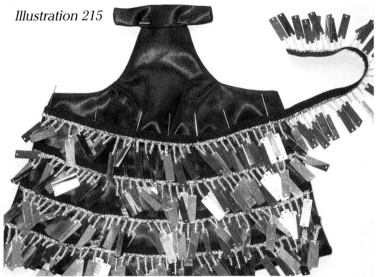

Illustration 216

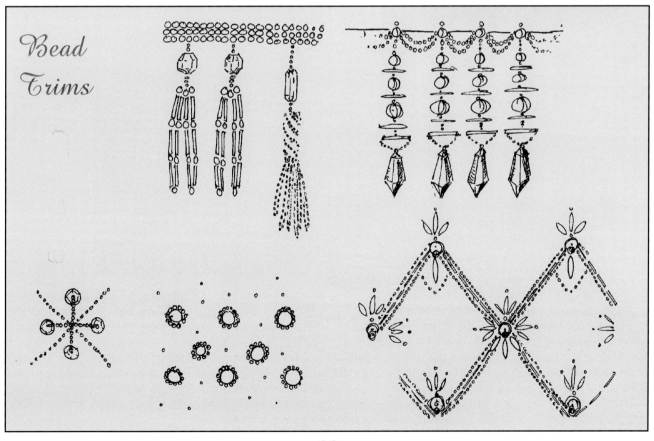

Bead Trims

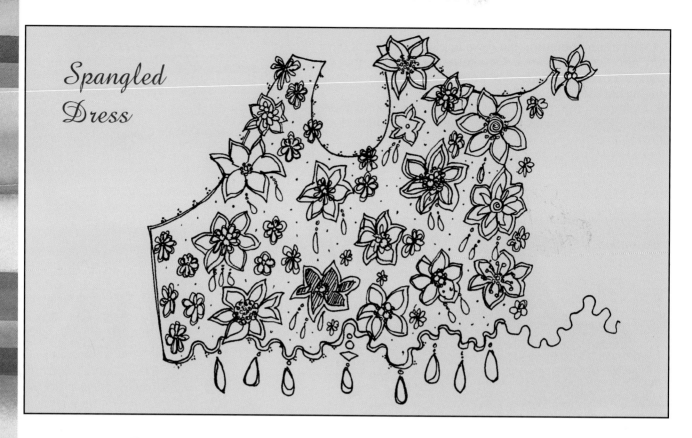

Spangled Dress

For the girls' stockings, I used a pair of unused white stockings for Daisy's® outfit, and a pair of girls black/silver sparkly tights for Willow's® stockings. Thrift shops often have drawers full of packets of unused tights, stockings, or pull-ups, usually in the most peculiar colours. Someone else's bad buy?! Ask. Your bound to hit the jackpot one day.

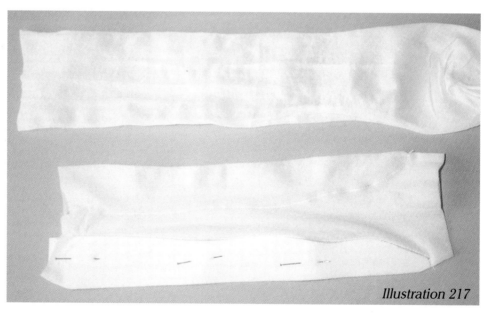

Illustration 217

Stockings:
Illustration 217

1. Place card template, made from the stocking pattern, inside leg of stocking, tights or pull-ups that have been cut to length of doll's leg. Place straight edge against fold and pin securely using fine bridal pins, so as not to leave an unsightly hole.

2. Then carefully machine stitch down edge taking care to follow contour of the template but trying not to catch template in stitching. If this does happen ease card slowly and carefully out of fabric, picking off the shards of paper once you've turned them. Repeat at other side.

3. Carefully cut out stockings trimming close to edge and turn to right side. Tops of stockings can be rolled or trimmed with small piece of lace taking care not to attach too tightly. In fact, it's best to fit lace while stocking is on the doll.

Contemporary Chic
c. 21st Century

Contemporary designers wrap, drape and structure fabric around the body looking to earlier designers for inspiration, re-working old styles, yet introducing a thoroughly modern style into them. Trend setters such as John Paul Gaultier, Vivienne Westwood, Versace, to name but a few, create concoctions of lamé, lace, gossamer frills, and swinging fringes. Yet underneath lurks some serious clothes that influence the fashion chain from couturiers to ready-to-wear down at street level.

Brocade Corset, Fitted Skirt with Kick Train

Star Rating **

Pattern Pieces:
TC1 Corset
TES1 Skirt Front
TES2 Skirt Back
TES3 Kick Train

For pattern pieces see pages 139-143

Materials:
¼ yard/meter brocade
¼ yard/meter silk dupion
¼ yard/meter coordinating chiffon
  interfacing
micro beads to match
materials for beaded head-dress as in
  Victorian section

Illustration 218

101

Brocade Corset
Illustration 219

This corset is made basically the same way as the corset in the Victorian outfit, however use the TC1 corset pattern for Alex®, Tyler® and Esme®.

1. Gather fabrics trims and beads which coordinate or contrast. *Illustration 220.*
2. Draw corset pattern onto fusible fabric (Bondaweb) and prepare stiff interfacing. *Illustration 221.*
3. Bond fusible fabric onto interfacing. *Illustration 222.*
4. Fuse corset shape onto brocade. Diagonal machine stitched lines can be worked to define shape and strengthen fabric. In real life-sized corsets boning is inserted to determine shape, which is too bulky a technique for dolls. *Ilustration 223.*
5. Cut around corset shape. *Illustration 224.*
6. Cut notches into curves, turn, then tack down. *Illustration 225.*
7. Cut lining to fit, and sticking to curves, sew lining in place by turning raw edges in and slipstitch in place. *Illustration 226.*

Illustration 219

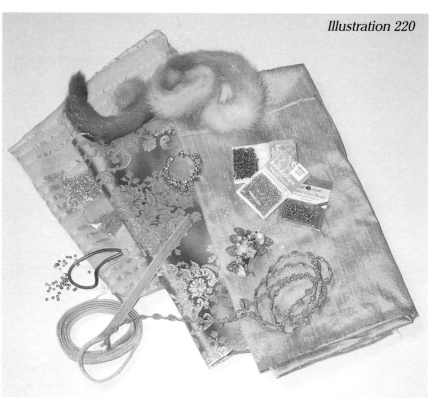

Illustration 220

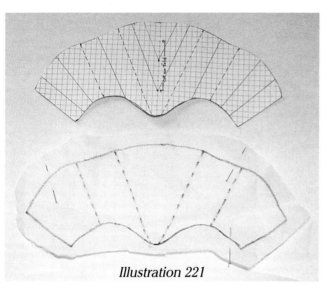

Illustration 221

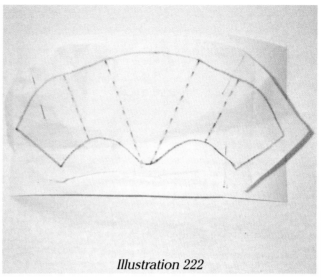

Illustration 222

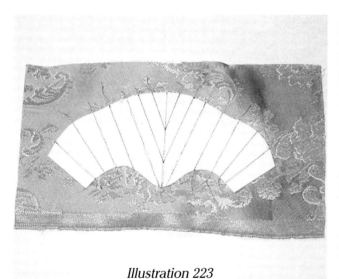

Illustration 223

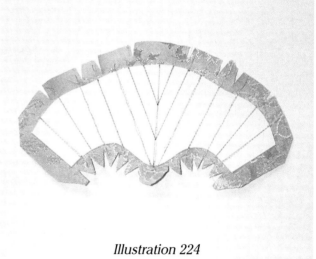

Illustration 224

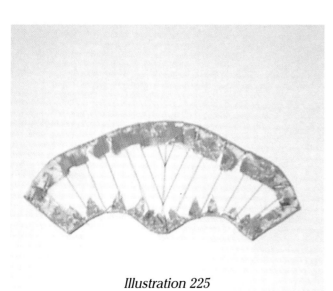

Illustration 225

Illustration 226

8. Finish corset on right side. *Illustration 227.*
9. Stitch hooks and eyes in place. *Illustration 228.*
10. Fit corset on doll. *Illustration 229.*
11. Add a small rectangle of fabric stitching in place just as in 1950's strapless dress to fill in gap in bodice if you prefer to have a more modest look. If not, do not add fabric. *Ilustration 230.*

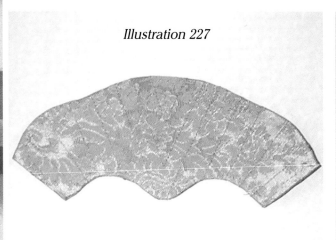

Illustration 227

Illustration 228

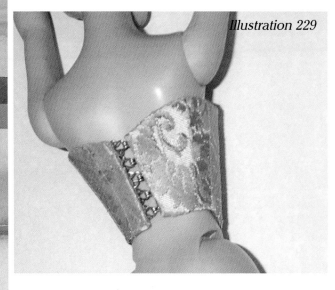

Illustration 229

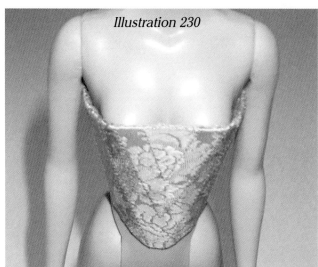

Illustration 230

Skirt

1. Cut front and backs from silk dupion and finish edges. Stitch in dart, and sew side seams.
2. Pin triangular train in place carefully matching dots as indicated on pattern. You may have to close by hand-stitching any tiny openings in the seam at base of center back opening and top of kick train.
3. Turn a hem on skirt and kick train.
4. Fold facing edges on center back opening and slipstitch in place. Turn edge on waistband and topstitch by machine. Mark for closures and sew press studs in place. There is no lining because I wanted a skin tight fit to the skirt and at the corset on waist, which will overlap onto the tummy, so any extra fabric would reduce the sleek look.
5. On inside of skirt using ladder stitch, pull center back seams together over kick train. *Illustration 231.*
6. Press skirt making sure train lies even at center back. *Ilustration 232.*
7. Sew press studs to back at opening.

Illustration 232

Illustration 231

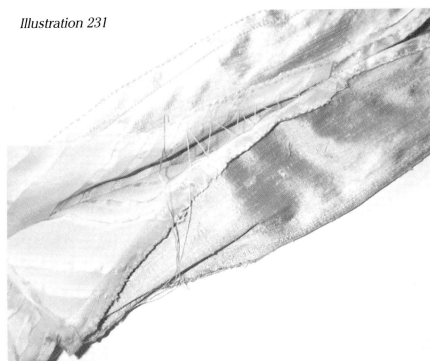

Illustration 233

Floral Headpiece
Illustration 233

Work head pieces as for Victorian head dress. This particular pin shown on Tyler® is the actual vintage pin I found in an old box of broken jewelry. It was dirty and crumpled, but I noticed the velvet flowers and beads, so I bought it for 10 pence, about 3 or 4 cents. I cleaned it and opened up the beaded flowers and leaves and arranged them in place. It's fairly fragile, but charming none the less. I examined it and saw it was just an arrangement of wired beaded flowers, velvet buds, and gold wire leaves bound together with florists tape with a tiny safety pin at the back. You could use a variety of flowers, leaves beads etc. to make your own headpiece to coordinate with whatever outfit you were making. Just use a little imagination

Beaded Choker

For basic supplies see *Illustration 234*.

1. Gather your beads and materials choosing colours that will contrast and compliment your fabrics, just as you would do when picking your own costume jewelry.

2. Sew two pieces of ribbon the length of your doll's neck in half and finish edges. Sew a press stud to each piece.

3. Next, measure around your doll's neck. Then gradually string beads or bugles between these pieces of ribbon working down each side. As you go increase strand by one bead to take into account the thickening of the neck towards shoulder.

4. On the last two rows, work some extra loops onto strands attaching crystals to center. Repeat with longer loops on bottom row. *Illustration 235.* Fasten off securely. Now try on your doll!

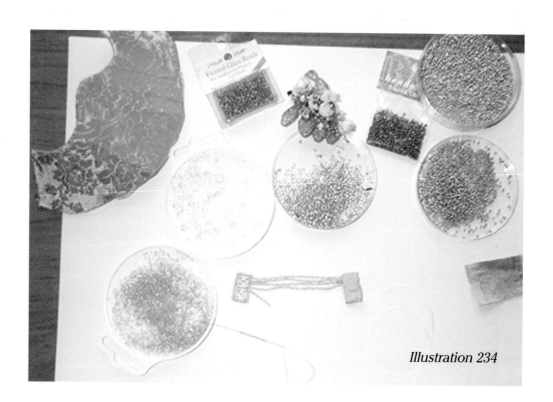

Illustration 234

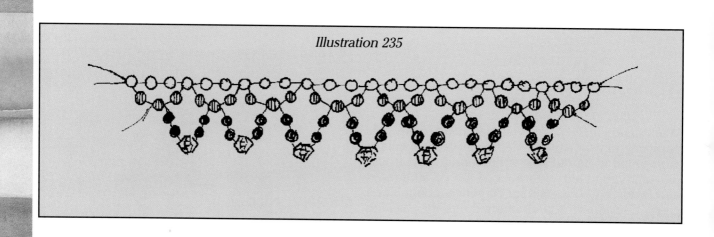

Illustration 235

Star Rating ***

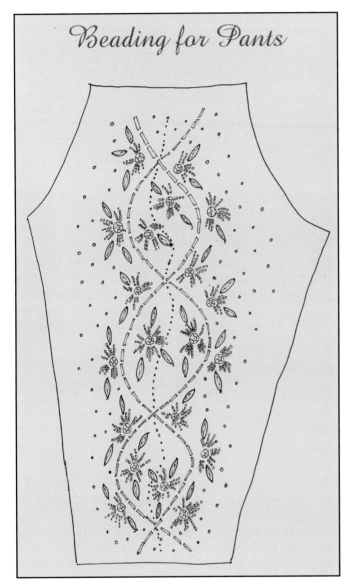

Beading for Pants

Illustration 236

Pattern Pieces:
TH1 Bodice
TH2 Halter Collar
TP1 Pants Front
TP2 Pants Back
TP3 Pants Facing

Materials:
¼ yard/meter silk dupion
¼ yard coordinating beaded or embroidered fabric
   for top
beads, sequins and bugles to match or contrast

Beaded Pants
Illustration 237

1. Cut out backs, fronts and finish raw edges. Sew side seams. Fold a small hem on center back edge, as in pattern. Turn hems on each leg and slipstitch in place.
2. Using beaded pattern as a guide only, bead each leg covering the side seam, but try not to get beads too close to either center front seam, waistline or inner leg seam.
3. When beading is complete, join center front seam. Then join each inner leg seam, leaving small opening at ankle to ease removal over doll's foot, and press carefully. Turn work carefully trying not to pull threads.
4. Finish all edges on waistline facing. Then, with right sides together, pin facing to pants at waistline and stitch in place. Turn to inside, press and topstitch along waistband line turning in edge at center back. Mark center backs for closure and sew on press studs going under crotch if need be for a good fit. Bead along waistline if desired and add any extra beads nearer seams just sewn.

Illustration 237

Illustration 238

Halter Bodice
Illustration 238

1. Cut bodice and contrast lining sewing in darts and press flat. With right sides together, stitch around edges from neckline, down back seams along waist-line, and up to neck edge. Do not stitch across neck edge because this will be left open to turn work to right side. Turn and press.
2. Fold halter collar in half with right sides together. Stitch each side between dots. Turn to right side and press.
3. Slip open edge over neck opening with right side of dress facing and stitch in place. Press seam and fold under raw edge on collar. Slipstitch open edge to wrong side of dress at throat. Sew hook and eye closure at back neck edge and press studs at center back edges.
4. Sew a fringe of beads to coordinate with beading on pants if desired.

Illustration 239

Illustration 240

Pattern Pieces:
A1 Alex Skirt Yoke Front
T1 Tyler Skirt Yoke Front
AT2 Skirt Yoke Sides
AT3 Skirt Dimensions

Illustration 241

Materials:
½ yard/meter shot silk
¼ yard/meter chiffon for wrap
20 gram ball angora yarn
one 50 gram ball finest weight chenille
3:3-¼:10 knitting pins
embroidery thread for embellishment,
   or at least 5 appliqué motifs
4in (10cm) strip brocade or other
   fabric for coordinating bottom band
beads to sew on skirt and chenille
   jacket

Illustration 242

Angora Sleeveless Polo Sweater
Illustration 242

1. With 3:3-¾:10 pins and angora yarn cast on 36sts.
2. Work 4 rows K1, P1 rib, increasing 12sts evenly across last row.
3. Work 12 rows straight st.st.
4. Divide work for armholes:
5. Knit across 12sts and turn, leaving remaining 36sts either on pin or slip onto stitch holder.
6. Working on these 12sts, decrease 1st at armhole edge, on next and every alternate row until 7sts remain.
7. Work 8 rows st.st.
8. Cast off 3sts at center back neck edge. Then work 5 rows st.st.
9. Cast off remaining 4sts.
10. Pick up first 12 sts from opposite side and work as for side completed reversing shaping.
11. Pick up central 24 sts and cast off 1st each end of next and following alt rows until 14 sts remain.
12. Work 8 rows st.st.
13. Slip central 6sts onto a safety pin and work each side neck edge of 4 sts separately
14. Work 5 rows st.st
15. Cast off.
16. Join shoulder seams and pick up Polo collar thus: Pick up 5 sts across back neck, 8 sts, across shoulder/side neck, 6 sts from safety pin, 8sts from side neck shoulder, 5 sts across back neck. 32 sts
17. Work 18 rows K1, P1 rib.
18. Cast off rib-wise.
18. Finish off all loose ends by sewing in or you could have knitted them in as you went along.
19. Mark for closures and sew press studs in place
20. Turn down Polo collar.
21. Press work very gently with a cool iron under a very damp cloth.

Illustration 243

Chenille Jacket
Illustration 243

1. With 3:3-¼:10 pins and chenille yarn, work as for Angora sweater up to the division for armholes.
2. Decrease 1 st at each end of work, which is now the front of your jacket, every 6 rows.
3. Work armholes as Angora sweater, but work center front decreases into pattern.
4. However, do not cast off center 6 sts in center of what is now the back section, but work 18 rows straight as for Angora sweater. Join shoulder seams.
5. Sleeves: Cast on 14sts and work 4 rows K1, P1 rib increasing 6sts evenly across last row, 20sts. Work 22 rows st.st increasing 1sts each end rows 6, 12, 18. Cast off 28sts.
6. Join sleeve seams and set sleeves in armholes. Press work lightly. Sew or crochet loops at center front edge and sew small buttons, pearls or bead clusters for closures. Then sew beads around entire front and neck edge.

Illustration 244

Full Skirt
Illustration 244

1. Sew darts in front and back section on both skirt yoke and lining. Trim edges and press.

2. Sew side seams; press open.

3. With right sides together, sew yokes beginning at bottom of one side working around waistband and down other side. Turn to right side and press. Topstitch along waistline edge.

4. Cut skirt to dimension given, finish side and top edges, and turn hem and slipstitch in place.

5. Embroider clusters of flowers or chosen design at intervals along bottom edge of skirt, or sew on appliqué motifs. Then add extra beads if desired.

6. Sew side seams; press open.

7. Attach skirt to front yoke by pinning each piece at center front point then folding tiny tucks around entire length working from center to each side until it fits yoke base. Stitch in place. Then press and slipstitch yoke lining over raw edges; mark back for closures and sew on press studs.

If you want to add a piece of lurex brocade fabric to base of skirt like green skirt shown, cut skirt fabric 4in (10cm) shorter than dimension piece and sew 4in (10 cm) panel of coordinating fabric to base. Finish and press seam, turn hem and continue as before. *Illustration 245.*

The floral pin was simply made with 3 silk petals, whose edges were dipped in fabric glue and then into poly-flake glitter. Then they were attached to a tiny gilt safety pin and pinned to doll's shoulder.

Illustration 245

Star Rating *

Illustration 246

Illustration 247

Pattern Pieces:
TC1 Skirt

Materials:
finest weight Lurex yarn, or similar
2.00mm/14 crochet hook
¼ yard/meter silk dupion
¼ yard/meter crinkle lurex fabric, organza or similar
five 3mm embroidery stones
bugle beads and large pearls for halter straps

Crochet bodice:
1. Using 2.00mm/14 crochet hook and lurex yarn work 36ch. Turn.
2. Work 2 rows sc., straight, turn and increase 1 sc, at each end of next row; turn and repeat last 3 rows twice. 42 sc. Finish off.
3. Find center point in work, join in yarn, and work 10 sc working away from center point to side.
4. Turn and work 1ch, work 9 sc, to end turn. Decrease 1sc, at each end of row until 4sc, remain.
5. Work 3 rows straight; then decrease 1sc, until 1ch left. Finish off leaving 15cm length of Lurex.
6. Work other side of bodice to match starting from center point again. Sew in any loose yarn leaving two long strands that will act as halter ties for your bodice.

Skirt:
1. Cut two rectangles of fabric as indicated on pattern. Finish edges and turn hem on skirt and lining.
2. Sew center back seams to point indicated. Sew lining inside of skirt along waistline.
3. Pin skirt to halter at center front points and gradually work little hand tucks along skirt waistline until it fits bodice. Sew in place.
4. Topstitch seam to bodice. Mark for closures on skirt and bodice and sew on press studs.
5. Stitch on embroidery stones along waistline seam. Then link each stone with strands of bugles in a combination of colours. Thread a few large beads onto halter straps knotting each end so beads don't slip off.

Ruffle Collar
1. Take a 4in x 1in (10cm x 2.5cm) strip of fabric used for main skirt and finish off raw edges. Sew a press stud to each end in middle.
2. Run a gathering thread along length in middle and pull to fit doll's neck making sure the press studs close at back. Fasten off securely.
3. Sew bugles along center of ruffle, and an embroidery stone to one side. Also add a few long strands of bugles with larger beads at end falling from stone.

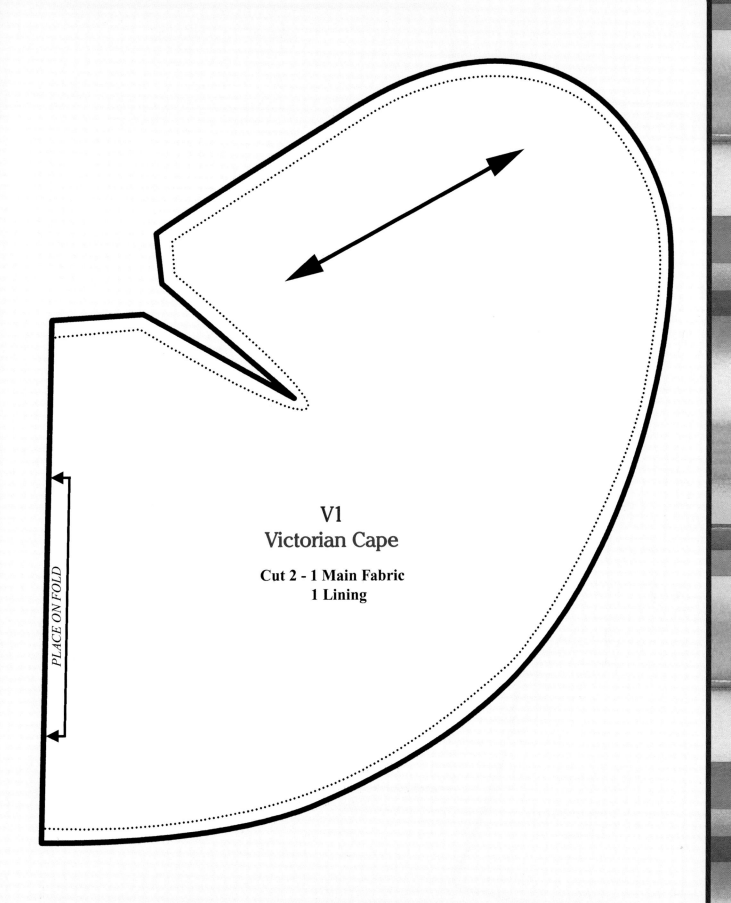

V1
Victorian Cape

**Cut 2 - 1 Main Fabric
1 Lining**

PLACE ON FOLD

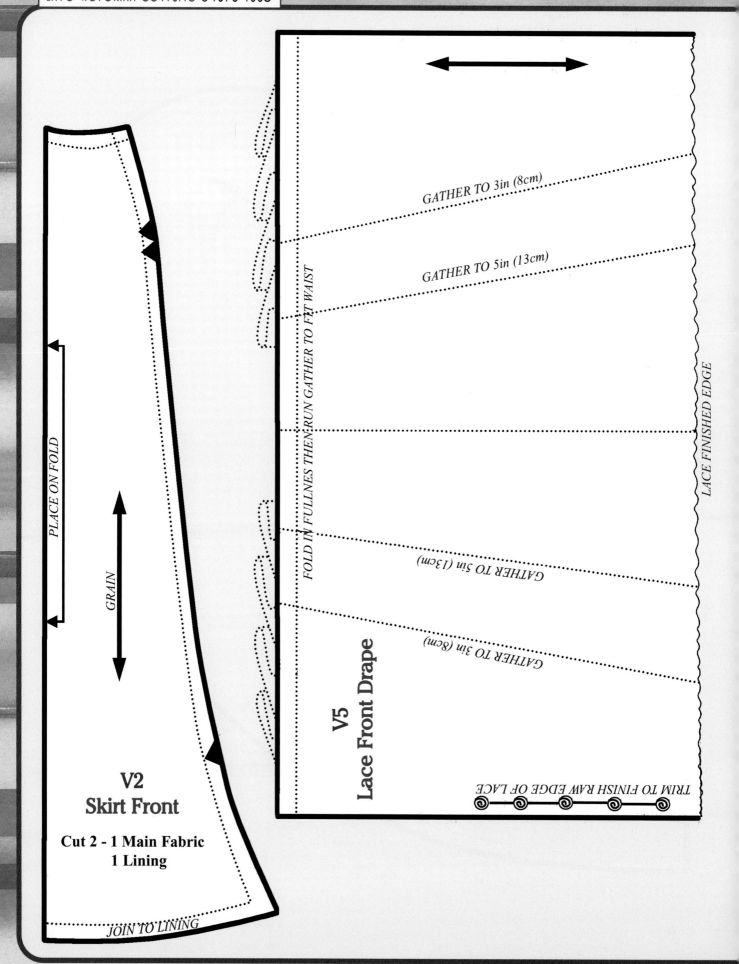

PLACE ON FOLD

GRAIN

V2
Skirt Front

Cut 2 - 1 Main Fabric
1 Lining

JOIN TO LINING

GATHER TO 3in (8cm)

GATHER TO 5in (13cm)

FOLD IN FULLNES THEN RUN GATHER TO FIT WAIST

LACE FINISHED EDGE

GATHER TO 5in (13cm)

GATHER TO 3in (8cm)

V5
Lace Front Drape

TRIM TO FINISH RAW EDGE OF LACE

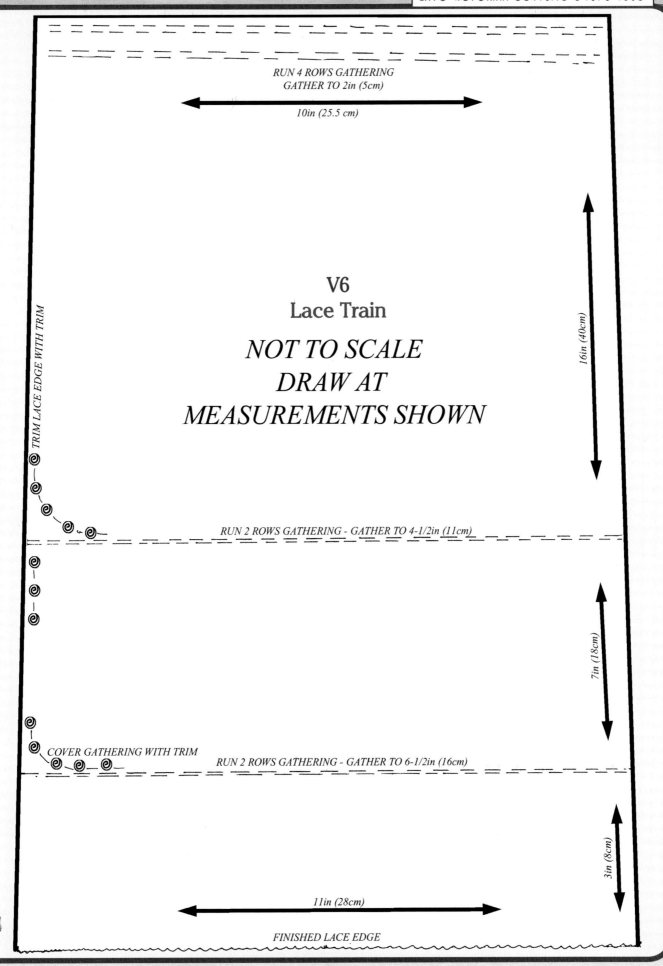

RUN 4 ROWS GATHERING
GATHER TO 2in (5cm)

10in (25.5 cm)

TRIM LACE EDGE WITH TRIM

V6
Lace Train

NOT TO SCALE
DRAW AT
MEASUREMENTS SHOWN

16in (40cm)

RUN 2 ROWS GATHERING - GATHER TO 4-1/2in (11cm)

7in (18cm)

COVER GATHERING WITH TRIM

RUN 2 ROWS GATHERING - GATHER TO 6-1/2in (16cm)

3in (8cm)

11in (28cm)

FINISHED LACE EDGE

*

*FOLD TO THIS POINT
TO REDUCE FULLNESS
AND CREATE MOCK BUSTLE*

B

V4
Skirt Back and
Side Combined

Cut 2 - Main Fabric
Cut 2 - Lining

JOIN TO FRONT

GRAIN

Match A & B to create entire pattern piece.

JOIN TO LINING

A

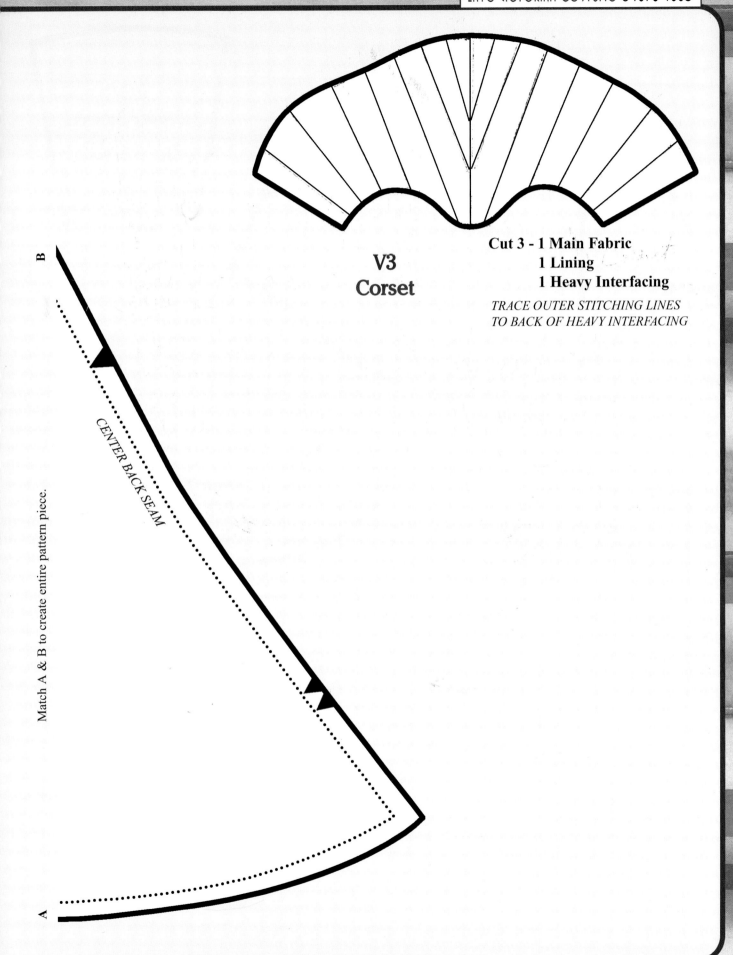

V3
Corset

Cut 3 - 1 Main Fabric
    1 Lining
    1 Heavy Interfacing

TRACE OUTER STITCHING LINES
TO BACK OF HEAVY INTERFACING

B

CENTER BACK SEAM

Match A & B to create entire pattern piece.

A

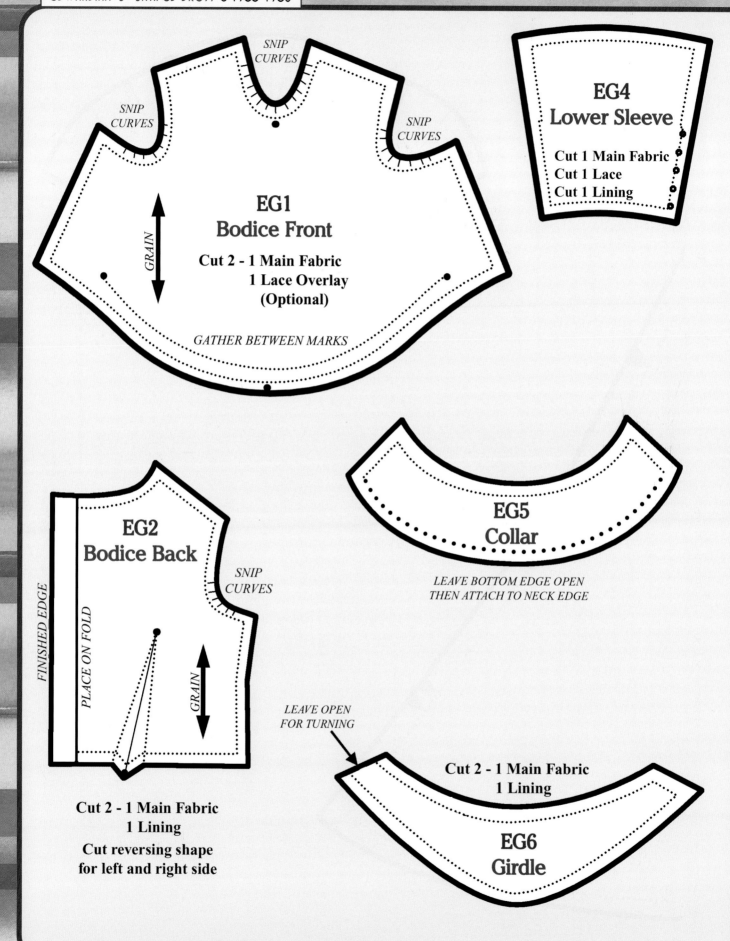

EG1
Bodice Front

Cut 2 - 1 Main Fabric
1 Lace Overlay
(Optional)

GRAIN

SNIP CURVES

GATHER BETWEEN MARKS

EG4
Lower Sleeve

Cut 1 Main Fabric
Cut 1 Lace
Cut 1 Lining

EG2
Bodice Back

FINISHED EDGE

PLACE ON FOLD

GRAIN

SNIP CURVES

Cut 2 - 1 Main Fabric
1 Lining
Cut reversing shape
for left and right side

EG5
Collar

LEAVE BOTTOM EDGE OPEN
THEN ATTACH TO NECK EDGE

LEAVE OPEN
FOR TURNING

Cut 2 - 1 Main Fabric
1 Lining

EG6
Girdle

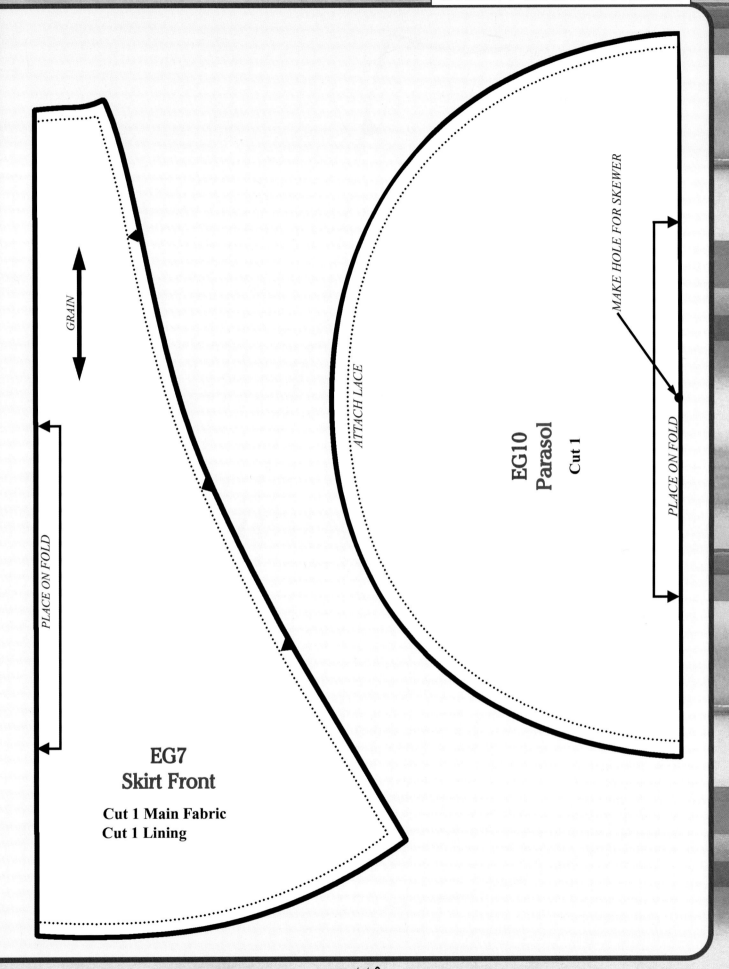

GRAIN

PLACE ON FOLD

EG7
Skirt Front

Cut 1 Main Fabric
Cut 1 Lining

ATTACH LACE

EG10
Parasol

Cut 1

MAKE HOLE FOR SKEWER

PLACE ON FOLD

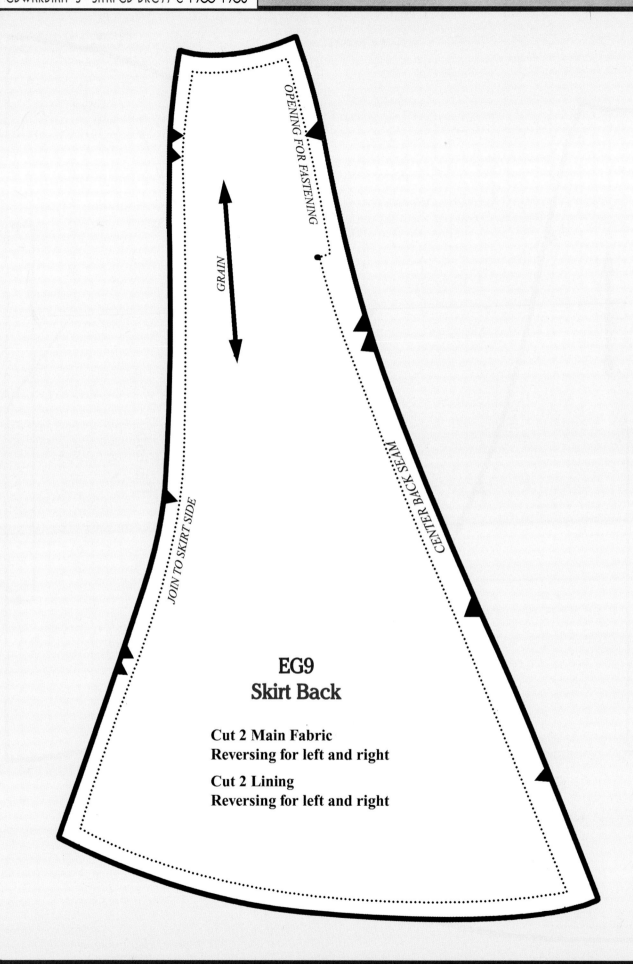

OPENING FOR FASTENING

GRAIN

JOIN TO SKIRT SIDE

CENTER BACK SEAM

**EG9
Skirt Back**

**Cut 2 Main Fabric
Reversing for left and right**

**Cut 2 Lining
Reversing for left and right**

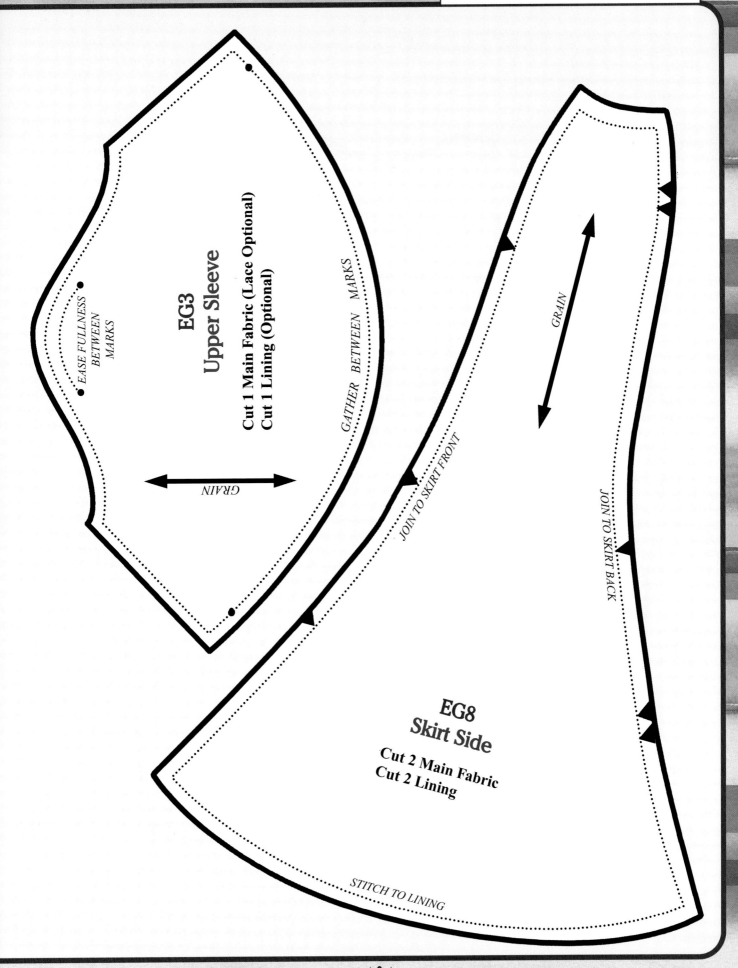

EG3
Upper Sleeve

Cut 1 Main Fabric (Lace Optional)
Cut 1 Lining (Optional)

EASE FULLNESS
BETWEEN
MARKS

GATHER BETWEEN MARKS

GRAIN

GRAIN

JOIN TO SKIRT FRONT

JOIN TO SKIRT BACK

EG8
Skirt Side

Cut 2 Main Fabric
Cut 2 Lining

STITCH TO LINING

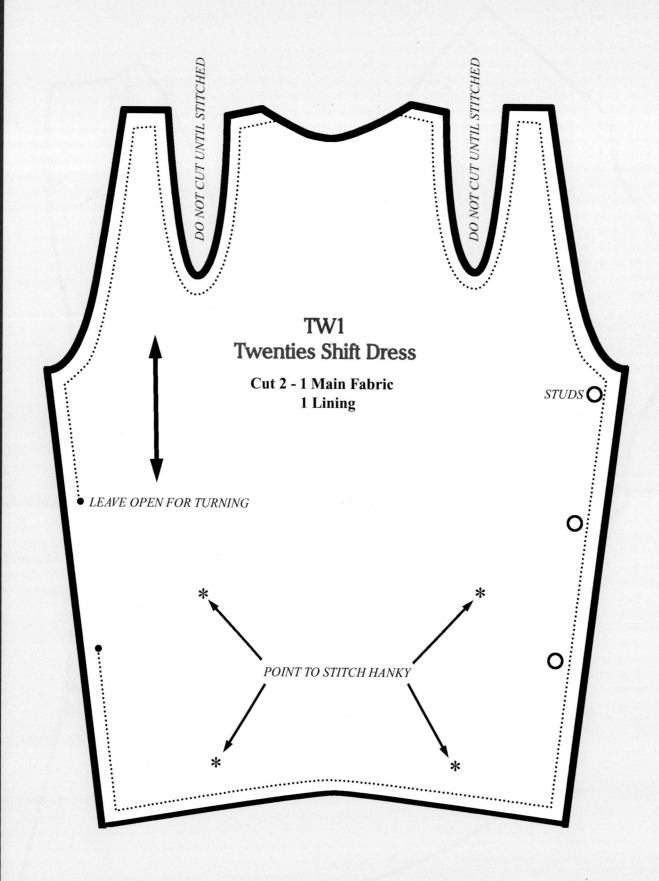

DO NOT CUT UNTIL STITCHED

DO NOT CUT UNTIL STITCHED

TW1
Twenties Shift Dress

Cut 2 - 1 Main Fabric
1 Lining

STUDS

LEAVE OPEN FOR TURNING

POINT TO STITCH HANKY

Cloche Hat Front

EYEBROW LENGTH

FLIP BRIM EDGE

Cloche Hat Back

EYEBROW LENGTH

FLIP BRIM EDGE

Cloche Hat Side

EYEBROW LENGTH

FLIP BRIM EDGE

Cloche Hat Side

EYEBROW LENGTH

FLIP BRIM EDGE

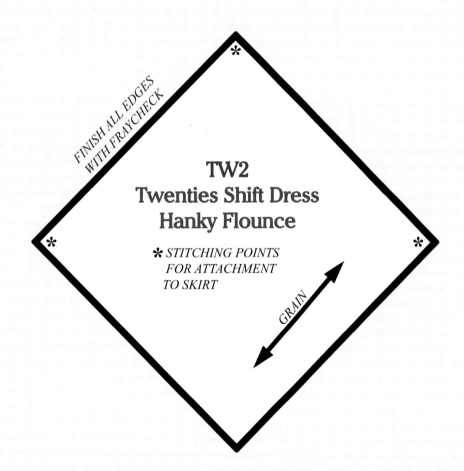

FINISH ALL EDGES WITH FRAYCHECK

**TW2
Twenties Shift Dress
Hanky Flounce**

✻ STITCHING POINTS FOR ATTACHMENT TO SKIRT

GRAIN

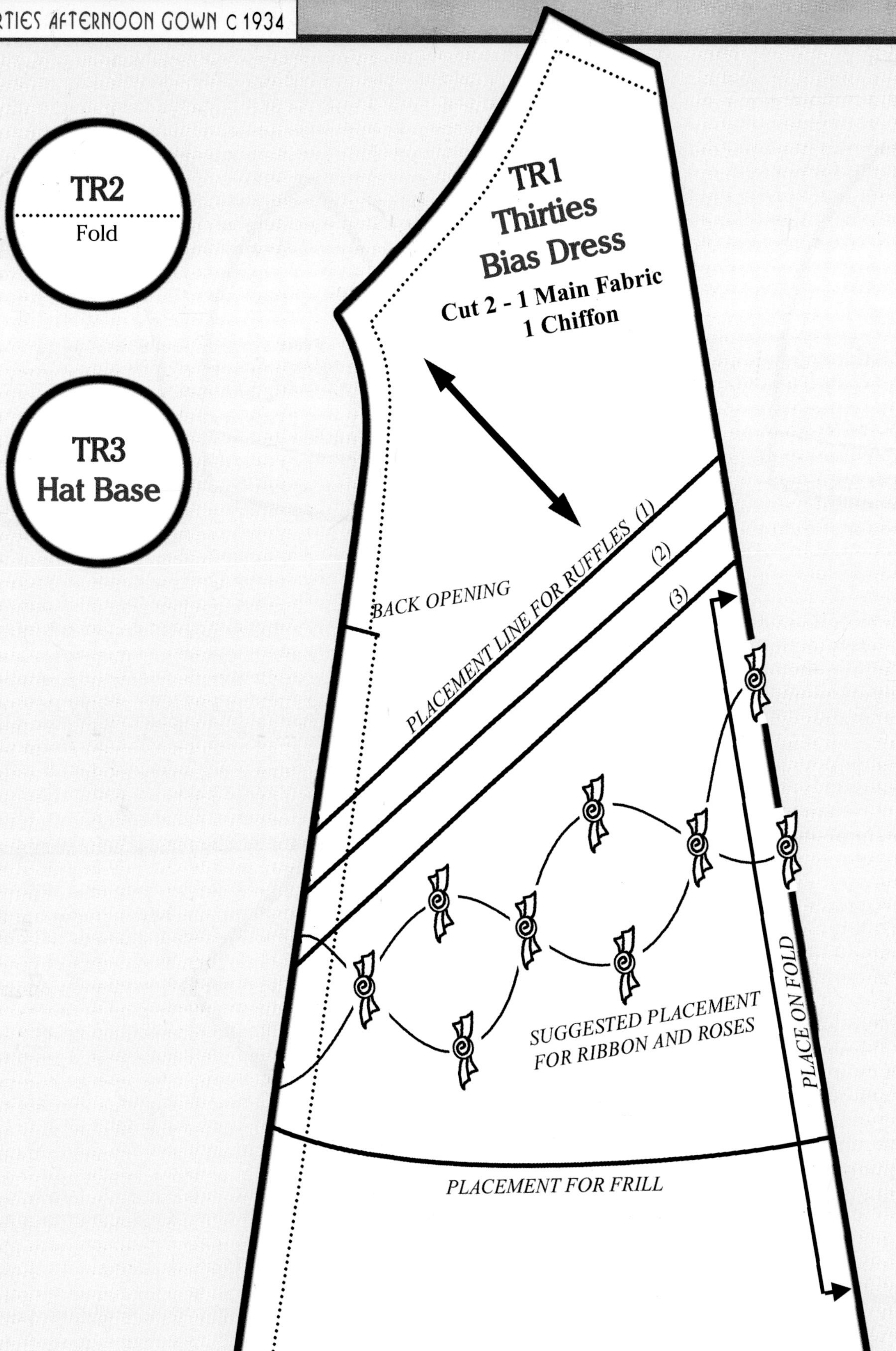

TR2
Fold

TR3
Hat Base

TR1
Thirties
Bias Dress
Cut 2 - 1 Main Fabric
1 Chiffon

BACK OPENING

PLACEMENT LINE FOR RUFFLES (1)

(2)

(3)

SUGGESTED PLACEMENT
FOR RIBBON AND ROSES

PLACE ON FOLD

PLACEMENT FOR FRILL

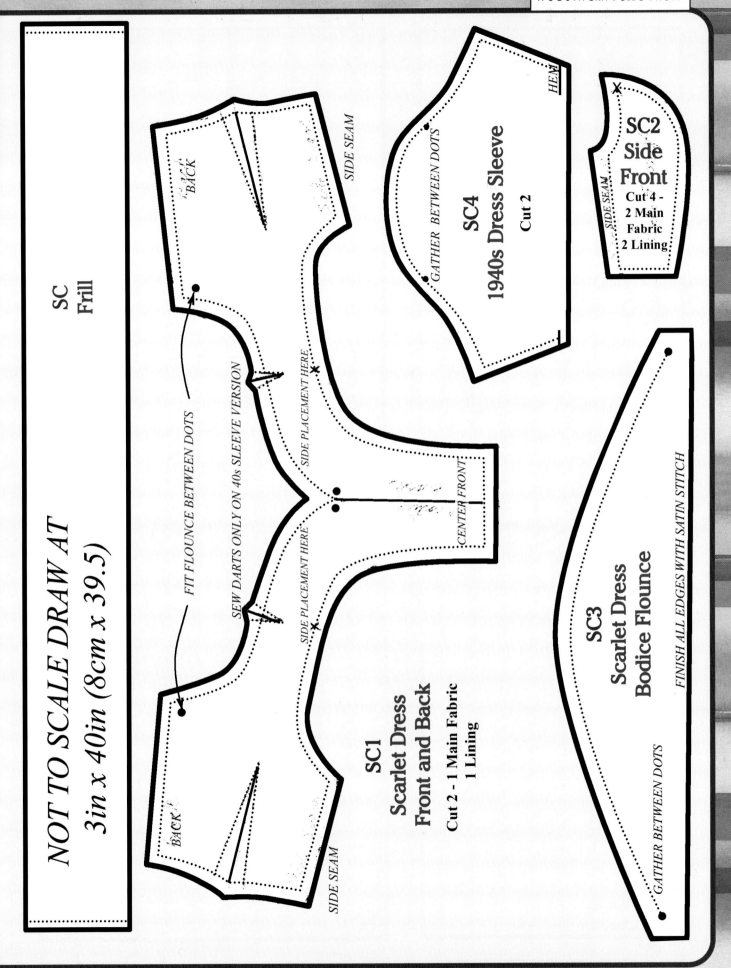

SC
Frill

NOT TO SCALE DRAW AT
3in x 40in (8cm x 39.5)

BACK

SIDE SEAM

FIT FLOUNCE BETWEEN DOTS

SEW DARTS ONLY ON 40s SLEEVE VERSION

SIDE PLACEMENT HERE

SIDE PLACEMENT HERE

CENTER FRONT

BACK

SIDE SEAM

SC1
**Scarlet Dress
Front and Back**

Cut 2 - 1 Main Fabric
1 Lining

GATHER BETWEEN DOTS

SIDE PLACEMENT HERE

HEM

SC4
1940s Dress Sleeve

Cut 2

SIDE SEAM

X

SC2
**Side
Front**

Cut 4 -
2 Main
Fabric
2 Lining

SC3
**Scarlet Dress
Bodice Flounce**

FINISH ALL EDGES WITH SATIN STITCH

GATHER BETWEEN DOTS

SC5
Scarlet Skirt
Cut 2 - 1 Main Fabric
1 Petticoat
NOT TO SCALE
DRAW AT
12in x 40in
(30cm x 39.5cm)

HEM FINISH WITH SATIN STITCH

5-1/2in
(14cm)

HEM

3in (8cm)

SC6
Scarlet Stripe
Skirt 1940s

Cut 1 Main Fabric

NOT TO SCALE
DRAW AT
10in x 26in
(25cm x 66cm)

HEM

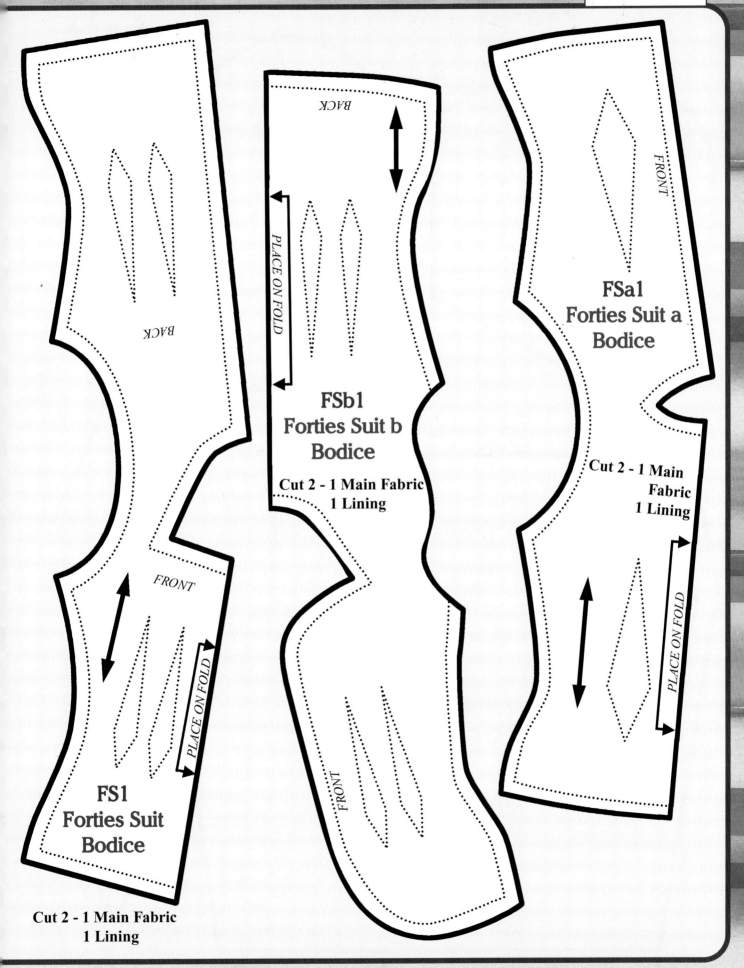

BACK

BACK

FRONT

**FS1
Forties Suit
Bodice**

**Cut 2 - 1 Main Fabric
1 Lining**

PLACE ON FOLD

BACK

PLACE ON FOLD

**FSb1
Forties Suit b
Bodice**

**Cut 2 - 1 Main Fabric
1 Lining**

FRONT

FRONT

**FSa1
Forties Suit a
Bodice**

**Cut 2 - 1 Main
Fabric
1 Lining**

PLACE ON FOLD

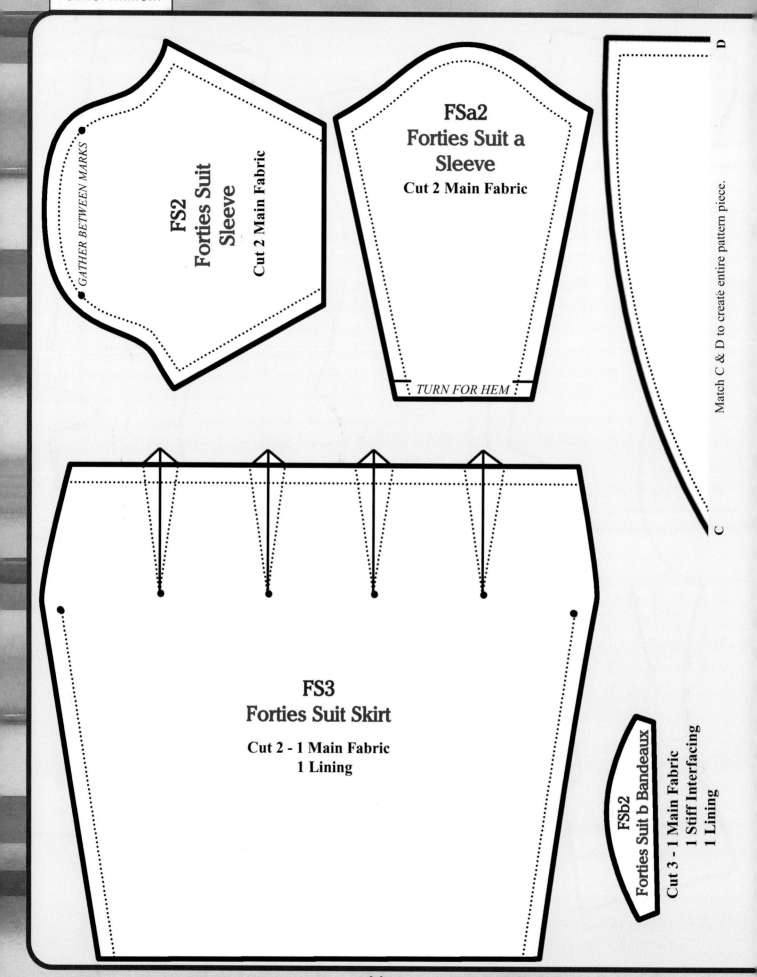

FS2
Forties Suit Sleeve
Cut 2 Main Fabric

GATHER BETWEEN MARKS

FSa2
Forties Suit a
Sleeve
Cut 2 Main Fabric

TURN FOR HEM

Match C & D to create entire pattern piece.

D

C

FS3
Forties Suit Skirt

Cut 2 - 1 Main Fabric
1 Lining

FSb2
Forties Suit b Bandeaux

Cut 3 - 1 Main Fabric
1 Stiff Interfacing
1 Lining

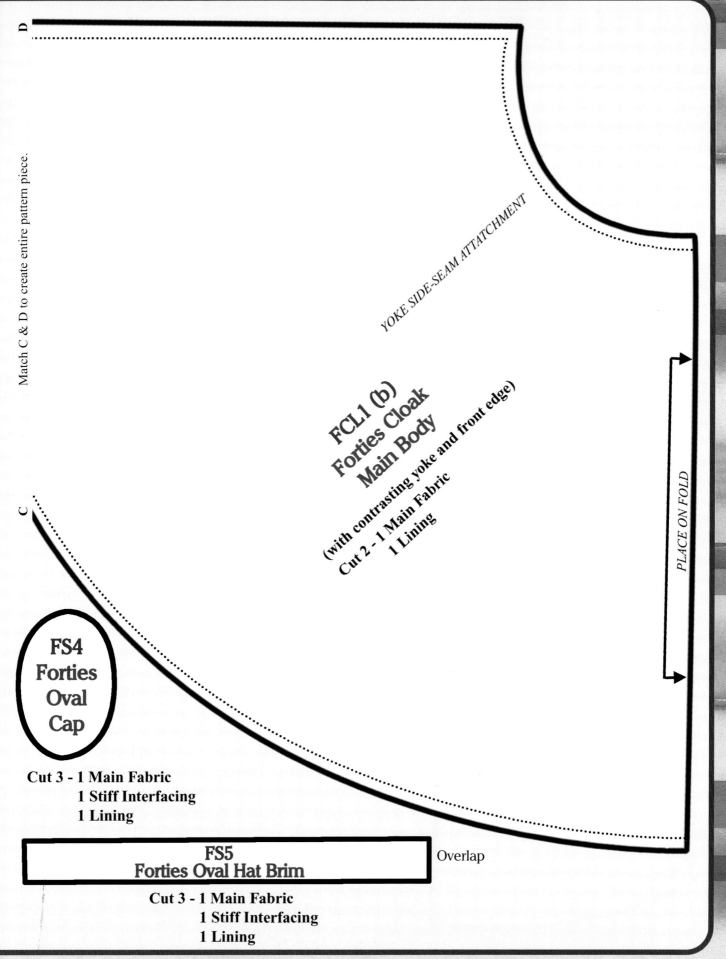

D

Match C & D to create entire pattern piece.

YOKE SIDE-SEAM ATTATCHMENT

FCL1 (b)
Forties Cloak
Main Body
(with contrasting yoke and front edge)
Cut 2 - 1 Main Fabric
1 Lining

PLACE ON FOLD

C

**FS4
Forties
Oval
Cap**

Cut 3 - 1 Main Fabric
1 Stiff Interfacing
1 Lining

**FS5
Forties Oval Hat Brim**

Overlap

Cut 3 - 1 Main Fabric
1 Stiff Interfacing
1 Lining

PLACE ON FOLD

F

Match E & F to create entire pattern piece.

**FCL1 (a)
Forties Cloak
Main Body**

(without contrasting edging)

**Cut 2 - 1 Main Fabric
1 Lining**

JOIN TO LINING - NO HEM

E

**FCL2 (a)
Forties Cloak
Front Yoke**

**Cut 4 - 2 Main Fabric
2 Lining
Reversing for
left and right sides**

PLACE ON FOLD

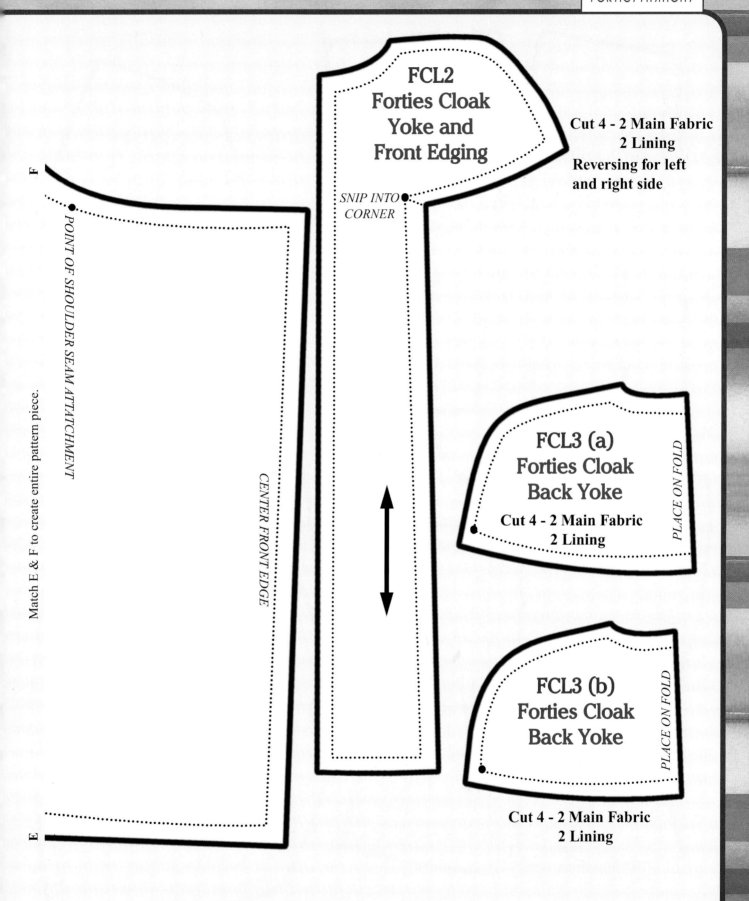

FCL2
Forties Cloak
Yoke and
Front Edging

Cut 4 - 2 Main Fabric
2 Lining
Reversing for left
and right side

SNIP INTO CORNER

POINT OF SHOULDER SEAM ATTATCHMENT

Match E & F to create entire pattern piece.

CENTER FRONT EDGE

F

E

FCL3 (a)
Forties Cloak
Back Yoke
Cut 4 - 2 Main Fabric
2 Lining

PLACE ON FOLD

FCL3 (b)
Forties Cloak
Back Yoke

PLACE ON FOLD

Cut 4 - 2 Main Fabric
2 Lining

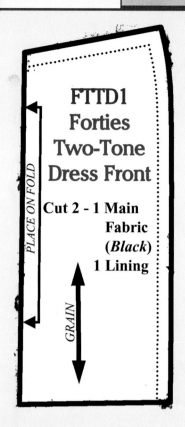

FTTD1
Forties Two-Tone Dress Front

Cut 2 - 1 Main Fabric (*Black*) 1 Lining

PLACE ON FOLD

GRAIN

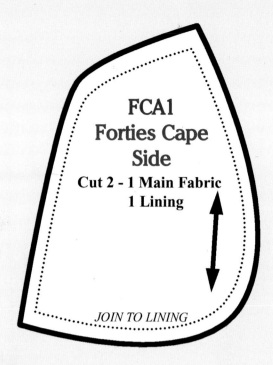

FTTD2
Forties Two-Tone Dress Back

Cut 4 - 2 Main Fabric 2 Lining Cut reversing shape for left and right sides

CENTER BACK SEAM

FCA1
Forties Cape Side

Cut 2 - 1 Main Fabric 1 Lining

JOIN TO LINING

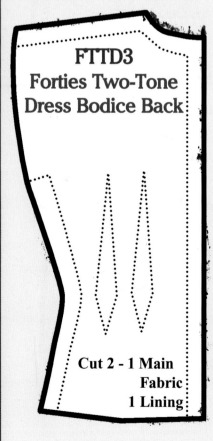

FTTD3
Forties Two-Tone Dress Bodice Back

Cut 2 - 1 Main Fabric 1 Lining

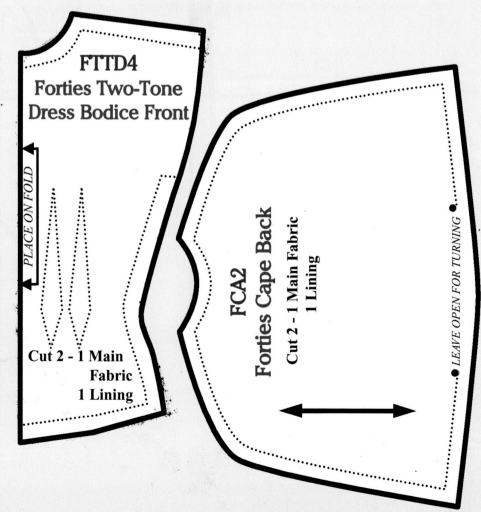

FTTD4
Forties Two-Tone Dress Bodice Front

PLACE ON FOLD

Cut 2 - 1 Main Fabric 1 Lining

FCA2
Forties Cape Back

Cut 2 - 1 Main Fabric 1 Lining

LEAVE OPEN FOR TURNING

BD3
Baby Dress Skirt
Straight Cut

Cut 1

NOT TO SCALE
DRAW AT
9in x 20in
(23cm x 51cm)

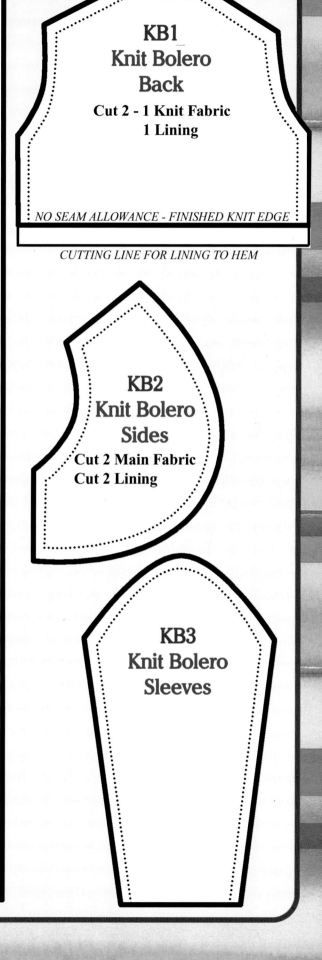

KB1
Knit Bolero
Back

Cut 2 - 1 Knit Fabric
1 Lining

NO SEAM ALLOWANCE - FINISHED KNIT EDGE

CUTTING LINE FOR LINING TO HEM

KB2
Knit Bolero
Sides
Cut 2 Main Fabric
Cut 2 Lining

KB3
Knit Bolero
Sleeves

PLACE ON FOLD

CENTER FRONT

H

BD1
Fifties Baby Dress Skirt
(Circular Cut)

Cut 2 - 1 Main Fabric
1 - Lining

JOIN TO LINING AFTER CLOSING BACK SEAM

Match G & H to create entire pattern piece.

PLACE ON FOLD

FJ2

**Fifties Strapless
Bodice Front**

G

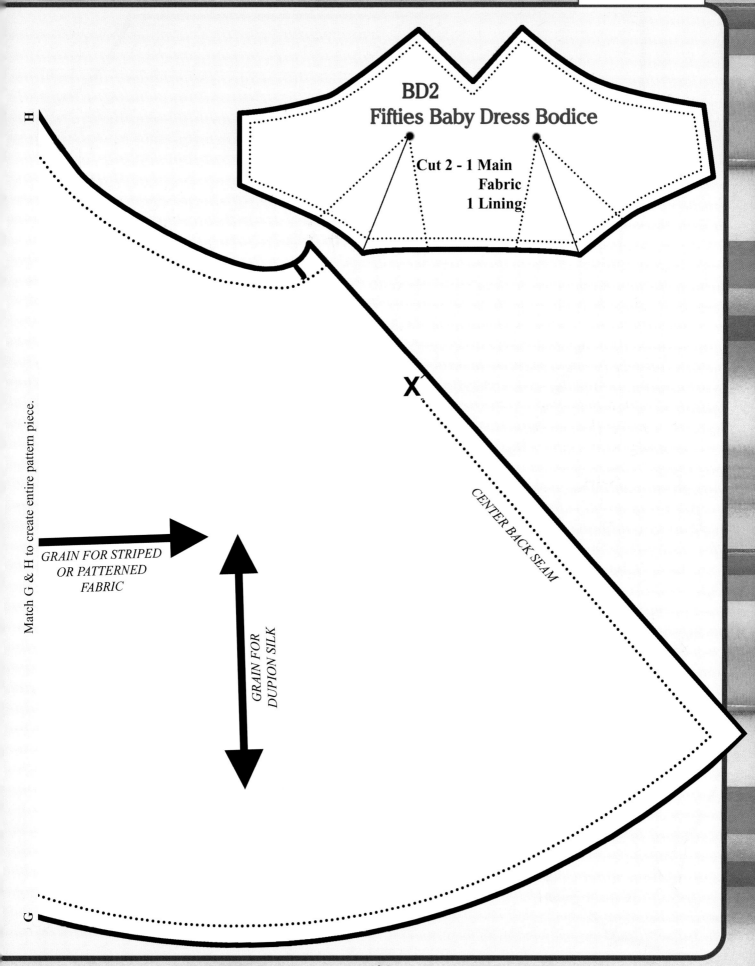

BD2
Fifties Baby Dress Bodice

Cut 2 - 1 Main
Fabric
1 Lining

H

Match G & H to create entire pattern piece.

GRAIN FOR STRIPED
OR PATTERNED
FABRIC

GRAIN FOR
DUPION SILK

CENTER BACK SEAM

X

G

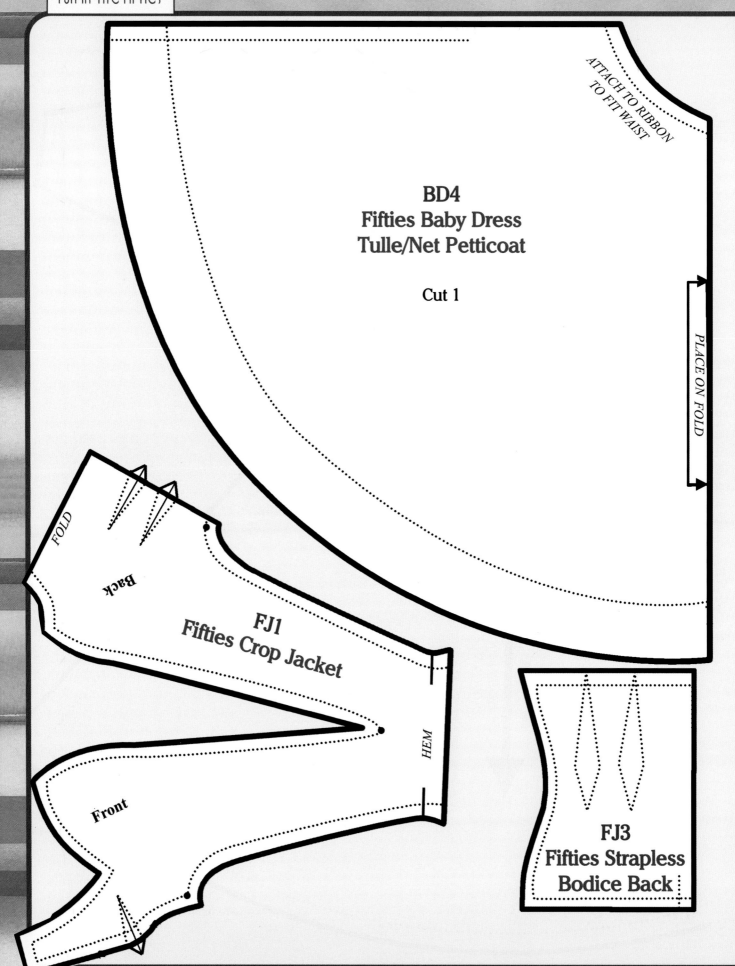

BD4
Fifties Baby Dress
Tulle/Net Petticoat

Cut 1

ATTACH TO RIBBON
TO FIT WAIST

PLACE ON FOLD

FJ1
Fifties Crop Jacket

FOLD

Back

Front

HEM

FJ3
Fifties Strapless
Bodice Back

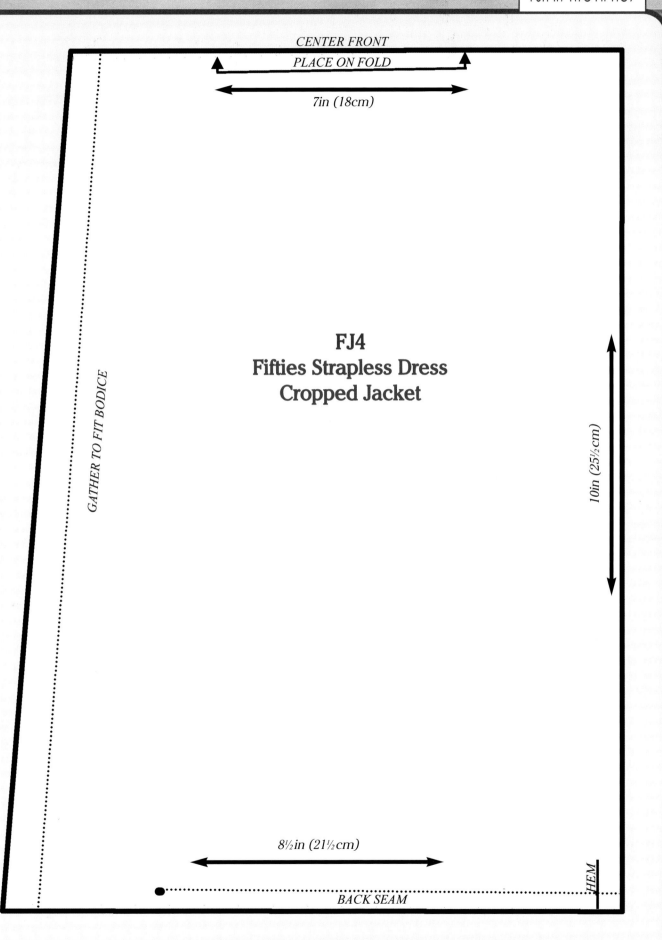

CENTER FRONT
PLACE ON FOLD

7in (18cm)

GATHER TO FIT BODICE

FJ4
Fifties Strapless Dress
Cropped Jacket

10in (25½cm)

8½in (21½cm)

HEM

BACK SEAM

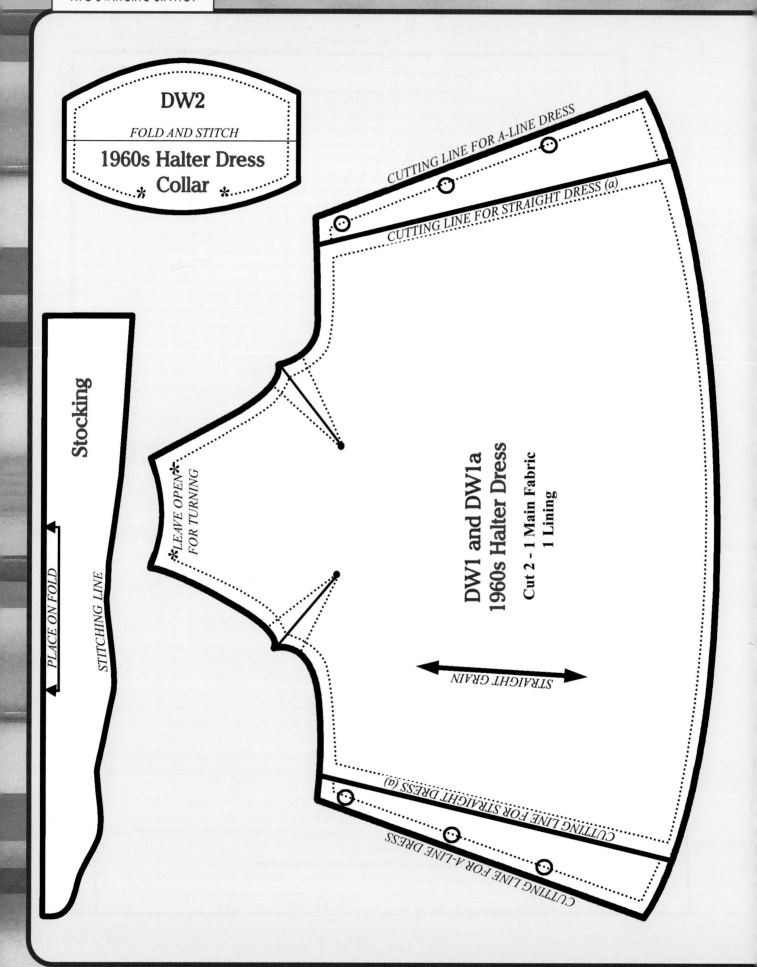

DW2

FOLD AND STITCH

**1960s Halter Dress
Collar**
❋   ❋

Stocking

PLACE ON FOLD

STITCHING LINE

❋ LEAVE OPEN
FOR TURNING

CUTTING LINE FOR A-LINE DRESS

CUTTING LINE FOR STRAIGHT DRESS *(a)*

**DW1 and DW1a
1960s Halter Dress**

**Cut 2 – 1 Main Fabric
1 Lining**

STRAIGHT GRAIN

CUTTING LINE FOR STRAIGHT DRESS *(a)*

CUTTING LINE FOR A-LINE DRESS

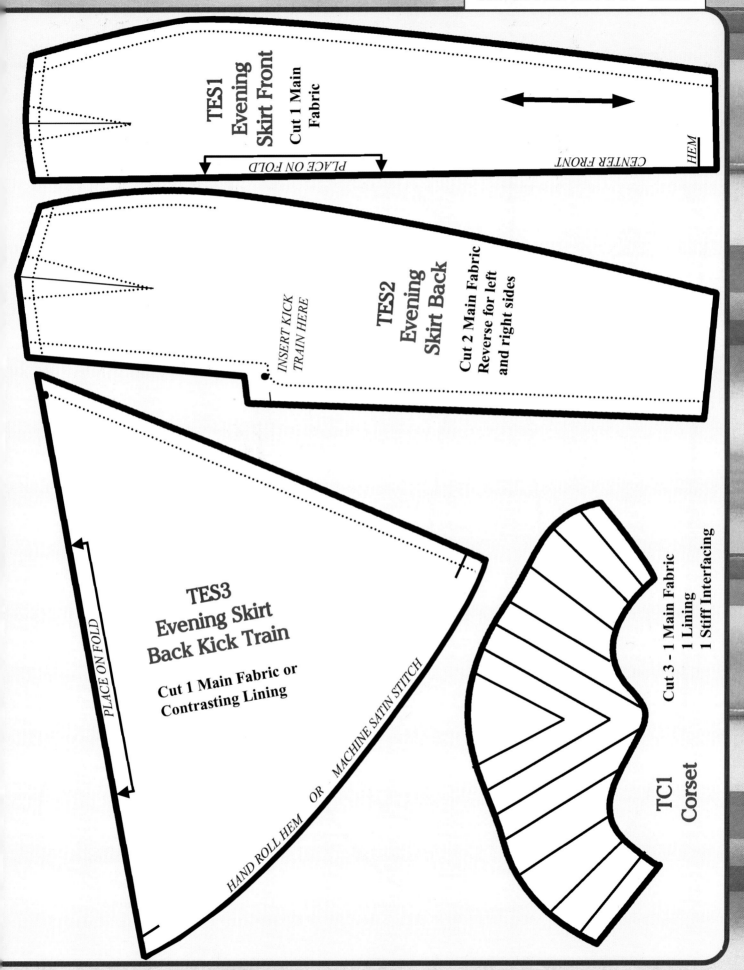

TES1
Evening Skirt Front
Cut 1 Main Fabric

PLACE ON FOLD

CENTER FRONT

HEM

TES2
Evening Skirt Back

Cut 2 Main Fabric
Reverse for left
and right sides

INSERT KICK TRAIN HERE

TES3
Evening Skirt Back Kick Train

Cut 1 Main Fabric or
Contrasting Lining

PLACE ON FOLD

HAND ROLL HEM OR MACHINE SATIN STITCH

TC1
Corset

Cut 3 - 1 Main Fabric
1 Lining
1 Stiff Interfacing

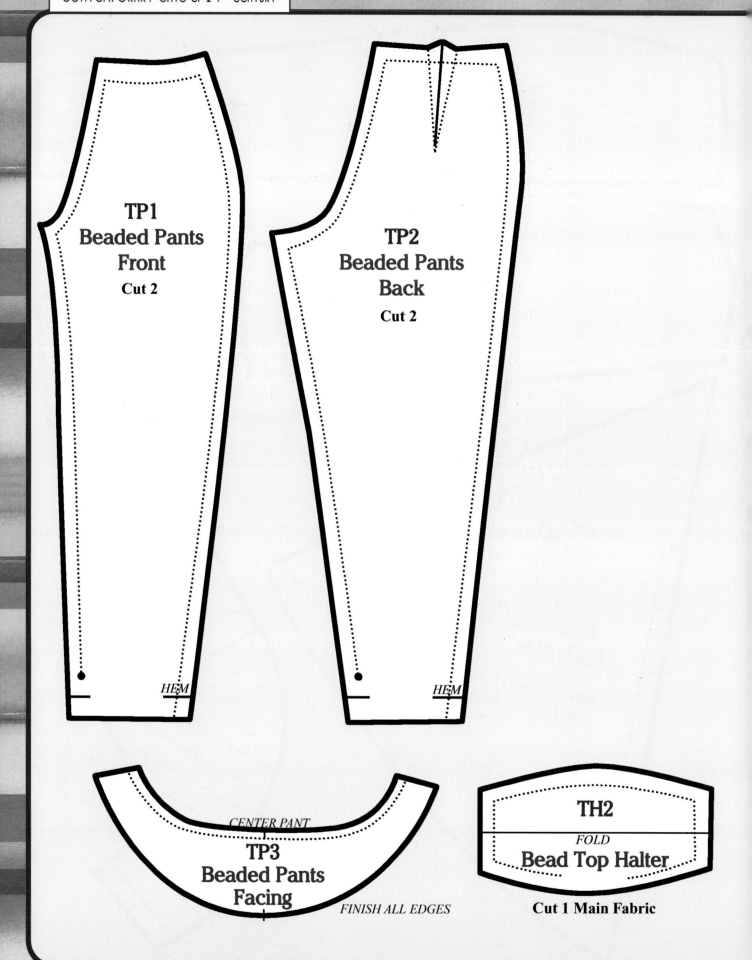

TP1
Beaded Pants
Front
Cut 2

TP2
Beaded Pants
Back
Cut 2

HEM

HEM

CENTER PANT

TP3
Beaded Pants
Facing

FINISH ALL EDGES

TH2

FOLD

Bead Top Halter

Cut 1 Main Fabric

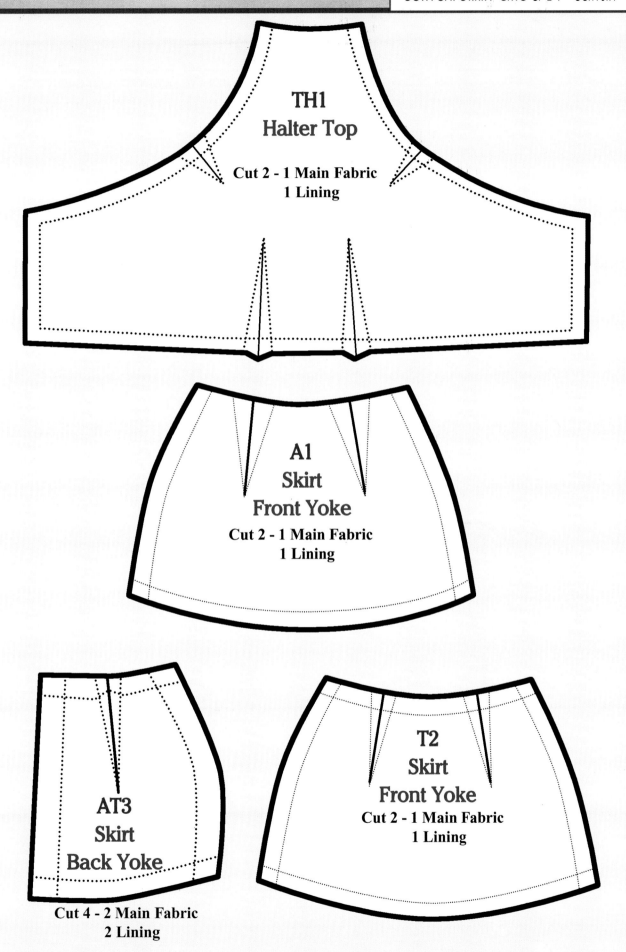

TH1
Halter Top

Cut 2 - 1 Main Fabric
1 Lining

A1
Skirt
Front Yoke

Cut 2 - 1 Main Fabric
1 Lining

AT3
Skirt
Back Yoke

Cut 4 - 2 Main Fabric
2 Lining

T2
Skirt
Front Yoke

Cut 2 - 1 Main Fabric
1 Lining

GATHER AND STITCH TO SKIRT YOKE

J

AT4
Skirt

Cut 1 on fold

NOT TO SCALE
DRAW AT
11in x 15-3/4in
(28cm x 40cm)

Match I & J to create entire pattern piece.

HEM

I

J

I

Match I & J to create entire pattern piece.

PLACE ON FOLD

TCH1
Crochet Halter Dress
Skirt

Cut 2 - 1 Main Fabric
1 Lining

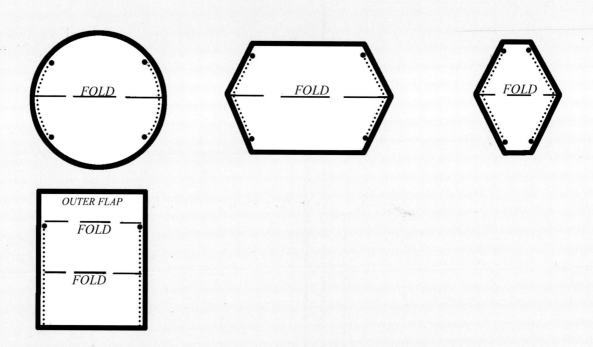

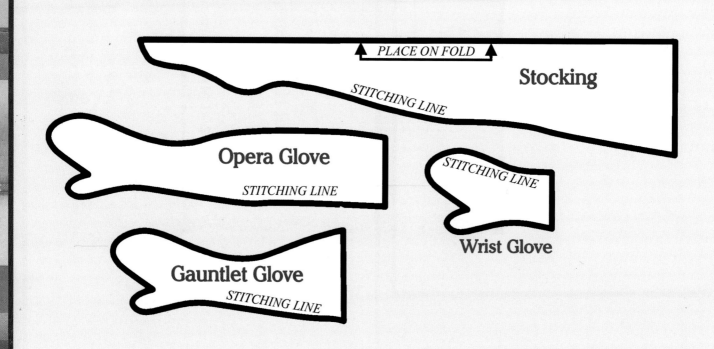